INFLUENCE AND INCOME ONLINE

Three Millennial Millionaires
Share Their Secrets

James Smiley
Steve Larsen and Josh Forti
and
27 Other Leading Entrepreneurs

Earning and income disclaimer

This book and its contents are for educational and informational purposes only. It is always recommended that you check with an accountant or attorney before acting on any information.

Regarding reliability, accuracy, timeliness, usefulness, adequacy, completeness, and/or suitability of information provided in this book, James Smiley, Marketing International LLC, its partners, associates, affiliates, consultants, and/or presenters make no warranties, guarantees, representations, or claims of any kind. Your results may vary. All claims or representations as to income earnings are not average earnings and should not be taken that way. Statements and claims in this book are not representative. You agree that James Smiley and/or Marketing International LLC is not responsible for the success or failure of your personal, business, health or financial decisions relating to any company products/ services. Earning potential is entirely dependent on the efforts, skills and application of the individual person.

Examples, stories, references, etc. should not be interpreted as testimonies and/ or examples of what an average reader can generally expect from the information. No representation in any part of this information are guarantees or promises of any kind. The author and publisher (James Smiley, Marketing International LLC or any representatives) shall in no way, under any circumstances, be held liable to any party (or damages arising directly or indirectly from any use of books, materials and or seminar trainings, which is provided "as is", and without warranties.

FREE

Your Extra Free Bonus Gift
($497 Value)

www.YourGiftFree.com

...act now to get your free membership to mentoring lessons from Steve Larsen, Josh Forti, and James Smiley

(Your free gift must be activated within the first 48 hours of your book delivery date or you may lose your discount. Take ACTION now... www.YourGfitFree.com)

(...no credit card or anything like that required if you act quickly.)

JAMES SMILEY

MOST IN DEMAND B2B DIGITAL MARKETER

 $210 MILLION IN SALES BEFORE 35

 3 FORTUNE 10'S CONSULTED

 12,521+ SALES REPS TRAINED

 560+ ENTREPRENEURS COACHED

 TWO $0-20 MILLION BUSINESSES

ABOUT

James has been recognized as one of the most innovative and in-demand entrepreneurs under 40. He has led $0 to $20M growth for two different companies, been a part of a Silicon Valley SaaS IPO, and consulted for 3 of the Fortune 10.

James has been the behind-the-scenes advisor to over 550 executives & entrepreneurs. His primary specialty is helping entrepreneurs with rapid revenue acceleration by leveraging online automations and his proprietary digital marketing systems.

James has published 8 books, recorded over 1000s videos and podcasts, trained over 12,000 B2B sales reps, delivered 600+ speeches, and sold over $210M before the age of 35.

HELPING ENTREPRENEURS
"ETHICALLY DOMINATE FOR PROFIT"

COMPANIES JAMES HAS SERVED...

 TOYOTA   Walmart :'< Google MOTOROLA

TESTIMONIALS

WHAT EXPERTS, EXECUTIVES, & CELEBRITIES SAY ABOUT JAMES

"James is one of the top under-40 entrepreneurs around today... get with him and listen to him!"

KEVIN HARRINGTON
TV STAR OF EMMY-AWARD WINNING TV SHOW "SHARK TANK",
FOUNDER OF THE INFOMERCIAL & AS SEEN ON TV

"The integrity and character James shows in business is hard to find and why he's one of the best in his industry."

JAMES MALINCHAK
TV STAR OF "SECRET MILLIONAIRE"
TOP FEE-PAID SPEAKER IN THE WORLD

"Once we started working with James, the ROI was immediate. He instantly opened doors that would have taken us years to get into."

JESSE DOUBEK
WORLDS #1 FACEBOOK EXPERT
CLIENTS: BRENDON BURCHARD, RUSSELL BRUNSON, & CHALENE JOHNSON

"James is THE BEST in the business at B2B Digital Marketing and High-Ticket Sales."

STEVE LARSEN
WORLD'S MOST IN-DEMAND
ONLINE FUNNEL STRATEGIST

"Working with James has helped me build an amazing online revenue generating platform."

JESSICA LYNCH
TV CELEBRITY
FORMER P.O.W

"My mind has been completely blown away after working with James. He's one of the best coaches and entrepreneurs out there for sure."

JOSH FORTI
TOP INFLUENCER MARKETER
7-FIG MILLENNIAL ENTREPRENEUR

TABLE OF CONTENTS

LEVERAGING INFLUENCE AND INCOME ONLINE

by James Smiley

*T**he following was a real interview James had with his $20,000 Platinum coaching students in a small group session. This information has never been shared before, and his students said this was the most valuable information they'd ever received.*

James, what's the story on how you made your first 6-figures at 20 years old?

(I was about 20 years old...)

ring ring ring... (I was calling my dad)

Hello, son, what's up?

DAD! You're not going to believe this!

What is it, son? Are you okay? Do you need me to come pick you up or something? What kind of trouble did you get into this time?

Ahhhh.... Dad, I just got a commission check, it's my first one.

And...? (said my dad)

It was for $16,000!

Son, I made $32,000 last year. No one is going to pay you $16,000 as a 20-something-year-old college dropout.

I think this is right, Dad. I was 300% above quota selling Blackberrys.

Son, listen to me! You're going to go to jail! DO NOT cash that check! No one is going to pay someone like you $16,000 for something called a "BLACK BERRY."

TECHNOLOGY = LEVERAGE

James, did that really happen?

lol Yes, it's a true story.

Where did you grow up?

I grew up in my impressionable years as an adolescent in Beacon Hill/Rainer Valley (south Seattle area). I grew up very poor and in rough parts of town.

James, if your parents didn't help you, did you have other family connections and that's how you made your money?

No. None of my family knew anything about what I was doing or how I was doing it. Lol

What were you selling when you first blew up financially?

I was a brand new B2B sales rep with zero experience, social proof, or connections. (You know, those things that most digital marketers make excuses about now.) I had those same constraints but didn't let it stop me.

I was one of the first people in the country to sell a Blackberry, and I just happened to be on the forefront of the smartphone, mobile, and digital revolution all in one (without knowing anything about it).

James, so honestly, how did you make so much money? Did you have a catch?

Yes, of course. What I've learned after making over $210 million in revenue (mostly from digital marketing) is that any time there's a massive increase in sales, there's *always* a catch. Meaning, there's something that the successful person did that other people didn't do.

So here was my catch…

I was sitting at my corporate desk (my first corporate job and my first B2B job), and I got the first laptop in my life. Remember, this was the year 2000, so there wasn't high-speed Internet like today.

My sales manager shows me an Excel spreadsheet (I'd never seen a spreadsheet before) with all my customers on it. There were 8,000 local businesses on my list that no one else in the office could reach out to but me. That was my list, they told me. In that spreadsheet were my clients' names, address, phone number, and email.

I was told to cold call 60 to 100 clients per day and speak to them on the phone about this flyer that was dropped off by a marketing lady. On that flyer was a promo for a "Blackberry" (which I'd never sold before).

About five minutes later, a guy from IT came to help me set up my corporate email (which I'd never used before). I'm not sure what got into me, but I had this revelation of sorts, like,

James, why don't you make your life easier and just email all 8,000 people at once vs. calling 100 people per day over 80 days?

So I asked the IT guy if I could do that, and he said,

"Listen kid, no one does that. Calling is the way it's always been done and the way it will always be done. People want to *talk* to you: they don't want to get your damn email. No one will ever buy from an email. In fact, kid, you'll probably get fired for emailing your clients."

...and then he left.

Well, heck...want to guess what I did next?

(Yes, I did!)

I copy and pasted all 8,000 emails into one email, grabbed the "corporate marketing approved" Blackberry flyer, typed it out into the email word for word, and hit the SEND button.

Then I was like... *Dang, that sucked.* Because nothing seemingly important happened; I was waiting for sparkles on the screen or an AOL sound or something.

I thought, *That was a waste; it didn't work.*

But guess what! Not 15 minutes later, my company phone rings and guess who it is? Yep! It was a client from my list calling to ask if I was James Smiley and if I could bring him four Blackberrys.

Let me make sure you understand what just happened. I just sold about 20% of my monthly quota in 15 minutes without leaving my chair or picking up the phone once.

And that was my dirty little secret to how I hit 300% almost every month. It was so easy that it was like cheating—but it wasn't.

It was LEVERAGE and this was the first time in my life that I realized...

TECHNOLOGY = LEVERAGE

I didn't need "connections"
I didn't need someone else's help
I didn't need a nest egg from Mom or Dad
I didn't need social proof or testimonials

Nope, I only needed to leverage technology.

James, what a story! How exactly would you say that applies to us entrepreneurs and digital marketers today?

Today it's the same storyline. The technology changes but the concept of leveraging technology to get ahead of the competition doesn't.

This narrative will never change, by the way. It will only pick up speed and change modalities faster and faster. Overall, the strategy will always remain the same. (As long as the Internet stays online.)

When you sell digital marketing, online automation, or online products to a client, you're not selling them a website, an online sales funnel, social media, or even your physical product.

You're giving them access to leverage.

Think about something common like Amazon. By using Amazon, I'm leveraging my money (good prices), their network (product selection), and my time (fast shipping).

Technology enables all of this leverage to happen and the leverage can be both ways many times as in the case of Amazon.

You see, if you're selling a physical product and you only see yourself as "selling a physical product online," that's exactly why you can't create maximum leverage. You don't see the other leverage points you're creating for yourself and your clients, thus you're not talking about the benefits that leverage will create, thus you and your clients are not able to capture the upside.

A broader example of how this applies today is that its been proven already that in over 90% of industries that the most underpriced leads come from online lead gen methods.

I'm not sure if you know this about business finance, but "cost per lead" is the most important metric of a successful startup. The startup who figures out the avenue to acquire the underpriced leads (aka cheaper leads than the market is seeing) has a very strategic advantage over all of the competition and much more latitude and flexibility long-term.

This is why webinars can be so hot right now. If you can get them to work, its over! Your cost per lead is so low (compared to other lead gen channels) that you can bankroll your entire business based on one great webinar script and generate enough cash flow to scale and grow from there.

Even if you're a digital marketer or a consultant, instead of saying, "Hi, I'm a digital marketer or a social media person," you can tell them you're here to see if they are interested in "using the Internet to get the most underpriced leads in the industry flowing to them."

What technologies today provide the maximum amount of leverage?

Without a doubt, social media and video. That's why I made the transition from being a "mobile first" and "mobile technology" consultant to a "social media consultant" around 2009/2010 because I saw the leverage in the world shifting from mobile to social, and I knew I had to stay out ahead of it if I valued my time, resources, and impact on the world.

If you look at what I do today and where the money is actually coming from, 90% of it is leveraging social media and video.

The other 10% or so of my income comes from talking to people by phone or in-person, but even then, 100% of those people are impacted and pre-framed before the meeting by my social media and video content.

It's safe to say that 100% of what I do today is social media and video driven.

James, what's the next big technology to leverage that isn't main-stream yet?

Without a doubt, virtual and augmented reality. But we are still years away from that, so if you haven't mastered social and video yet, don't worry about it.

James, did digital marketing always play a big role in all your $200+ million in sales?

Yes, but for the first 5 to 8 years, I hardly told anyone because I thought I was going to get fired or go to jail. Everyone told me it was cheating, but I knew it wasn't. They just didn't understand it yet, but I knew sooner or later they would.

Did people always disbelieve you when it came to technology?

Yeah, the "believability curve" went something like this (this is actually a true story):

> In my early 20s, I walked into a business, spoke to the CEO, and said, "Sir, in two years, all of your employees will be doing email on their phones over their PCs." The CEO laughed at me and kicked me out.
>
> Two years later, I walked back into the same CEO's office and said, "Sir, you see, now everyone is using email on their phones. Well guess what, in two more years, everyone is going to be using text messaging more than making phone calls." The CEO laughed and kicked me out.
>
> Two years after that, I walked in and said, "Sir, every one of your employees now texts more than they talk on the phone. Now, sir, every one of your clients will want you to reach them on social media instead of making cold calls." The CEO laughed at me still and kicked me out.
>
> One year later, I went to see the same CEO, but his business had gone bankrupt. Now, the CEO is one of my Platinum Coaching clients.

In any market, only about 10% are early adopters, so if you're selling a cutting-edge product or service, don't worry when 90% of the people laugh at you because the other 10% will buy like fire.

LEVERAGE = ALL IN

James, how much of a role should social media play in entrepreneurship today?

Look, the game of leverage is an "all-in" strategy. There is no strategic advantage to creating only 80% leverage. That's like a company thinking there is a strategic advantage to being the #2 or #3 priced product on the shelf. It's proven that those are the first products that retail stores eliminate.

Toys"R"Us was #1 until Amazon took over the toy market. They then thought, *It's okay, we'll be a high-priced #2."* Only 18 months later, they declared bankruptcy.

They should have innovated their way back to #1 to become the "Ross of Toys" or something like that.

In your world (digital marketing, entrepreneurship, etc.), since all of the leverage is around social media and video, you need to be all-in on that or you're not going to make it. Honestly, most of you won't even successfully launch because you're not all-in on this.

The future of what you do will completely be around creating leverage on social media and video, meaning that, essentially, you'll need to become 50% a media company and 50% your core value proposition.

My first hire on my team was Tracey, who runs social media and video for us. My next hire was someone who runs the operations of our core practice.

This is a great recipe for dynamic growth: publish everything you know and do not hold back.

If I publish everything I know, won't my prospects steal my ideas?

It seems like they would, but honestly, 98% of the time they won't.

Here's how to look at it:

About 98% of the people listening either (a) have a full time job and no time to do what you're saying, but they get caught up taking notes because they realize the value you're dropping, and they know they need to do something about it, but after you drop so much value, they throw up their hands and say, "I need this, but I'll never be able to do this" (which is the truth of the matter anyway, you just helped them get there quicker) or (b) they don't have the abilities or skillsets to actually execute what you're talking about.

So what about the other 2%?

I'm going to be honest. There are 2% of the people who are skilled enough and who will find the time to steal your ideas, but that's the thing about those people... People with super high IQs are not likely to join your program or they are smart enough to know when they're getting in over their heads (even if they could do it themselves), so just out of convenience and to save time, they'll hire you.

Remember, your goal is not to make your content unhackable; your goal is to make your content so rich and powerful that people feel like they can't do it themselves or, at a minimum, they feel like they need your help to get started.

This is true content marketing, by the way.

So, in a 10-minute video presentation that I'm going to do live on social media (or that I'm going to pre-record and post on social media), what should my top goals be?

Current I do anywhere from one to four podcasts or interviews of some sort per week. I have two goals every time:

1. Add so much value that the listener takes at least ten pages of notes. (I literally write out notes to myself on systems I'm going to share, processes I'm going to share, ideas and strategies I'm going to share, etc. And I make sure I drop all that knowledge, even if I have to interrupt the host at the end to get in my last five to eight minutes of value.)

2. Have a call-to-action that involves "takeaway selling." (You see, 99.9% of people getting interviewed are going to try to sell something or push listeners to an optin (which is fine). But I've found that the higher-value listeners usually will not optin to a lot of things unless they are really sold on it. But you can trigger these higher-value buyers by "takeaway selling" them. An example would be if at the end of a show the host says, "James, where should people go to follow you" and I respond with, "You know, we are so slammed right now that the best thing would be to follow you (the host) at (their website). I'm sure (host name) will be able to guide you to success. But, if you're serious and in need of help right now, you can find me and follow up with me here: (my url)."

Do you see how that would make a lurking higher-value listener think, *This isn't for everyone; this is for people like me who are elite.*

You'd be surprised how well that works.

Okay, I get it that I should be all-in on social media and video. But let's get real, James, how do I do that and still run my business, design the product, do customer service, etc?

Easy!

First, separate your days into content days, meeting days, and general business days. This is what we do, and it works like a charm. On a content day, they only thing I do is work on content and the distribution of that content.

A lot of my top students start to learn about my personal schedule the longer they are with me. They realize that I only work Tuesday, Wednesday, and Thursday. Monday and Friday and the weekends are flex days for me. I usually have my kids every Friday, Saturday, Sunday, and Monday, so I only work from 9:00 p.m. to 2:00 a.m. those days. (Yes, I'm a night owl.)

And the Tuesday/Wednesday/Thursdays are the only days of the week that I book meetings and do coaching calls. If someone wants to book me for a podcast interview, they can only book it on an opening on one of those days.

A lot of times, Mondays and Fridays are general business days for me where I'm answering email, Voxes, and PMs or creating a product or something like that.

What I'm saying is batch everything, and you'll be fine. It works great.

Trying to do it all in the same day is when you get screwed because you're forcing yourself to use different parts of the brain very intensely on the same day and that only causes your productivity to decline.

LEVERAGE = "X"

James, what are the best things for me to leverage even if I'm brand new?

This is an easy one, and every one of you should know this off the top of your head. You want to leverage "other people's X", meaning, you want to learn to leverage stuff other people have or own because they've already developed it, researched it, built it, etc., so for you to reinvent the wheel is the opposite of leverage.

Other People's "X" (we also call this OPX) includes other people's:

- time

- money

- resources

- events

- content

- book content

- information

- database

- knowledge

- network

- intellectual property

- background

- connections

- history

- relationships

- brand

- equity

- social proof

- and much more

Can you give some real life examples of how to leverage some of these?

Sure. Let's say you're starting out selling digital marketing as an agency to local businesses. Finding someone to partner with during your launch (e.g. a local CPA, local website developer, or a local gorilla marketer who markets with door hanger flyers), would be a great way to launch and scale quickly because you can leverage "other people's existing relationships, network, list, trust with clients, brand, history they have with those clients, etc.

If you did an email blast and dropped outbound voice notes to people's phone numbers (using a service like DialMyCalls.com) that is another way to leverage "other people's lists.

Here's another example. Let's say you're trying to sell something to school districts. That is a very B2B type of market, and there are a ton of roadblocks that will keep you from getting in there. Instead of trying to build in-roads yourself, leverage something already there such as try to find people who already do services with that school. Help those people and quickly they'll say something like, "If you ever need anything, let me know." Then you ask them to help you get an introduction to the principle (leveraging that person's network, relationships, etc.) but also ask them how to approach the principle (leveraging the person's knowledge, history, etc.).

Another example: Let's say you're a software company with a new CRM software for life and business coaches. The best place to start selling would be to sell an influencer who is currently mentoring fifty coaches. Do a joint-venture partnership with that person, give them maybe 30% of your sales, and let him promote you to his coaches, do a Facebook Live inside their private-members-only Facebook Group, and send promotion emails to his list. This is leveraging "other people's database, social proof, brand equity, relationships, etc.".

Remember, the ponds with your fish already exist. Trying to find your own clients to get started is like trying to build your own pond in your backyard (when you're not a professional pond builder) and then trying to find fish to put into it, and then you still have to catch them even though they are in your own pond. If you're a big company or you have capital investments, knock yourself out because that's what that money is for. But if you don't, creating leverage is the only way to go about it.

LEVERAGE = BALANCE

James, isn't leveraging someone "manipulation?"

Yes, but only if you're not allowing them to leverage you with equal weight. For instance, if an established influencer is letting you use their list of buyers so you can market to them, but you're not going to pay the influencer (or you won't pay them well), then you're out-leveraging that person and they will sense it and the deal won't happen or you'll have an unhappy partner.

This is how you get a bad reputation (because you get stingy and try to take advantage of people). If you keep the leverage balanced, you'll never be accused of manipulation or taking advantage of someone.

With that in mind, how do we keep the leverage balanced?

Easy, stop thinking about yourself, our product, and how much money YOU can make from the other person. If you start off the conversation by thinking, *What does this person want?* then you'll be on the right track and the other person won't feel weird about it.

If they are getting weirded out, it's because you are not doing a good enough job of thinking about them, their business, and their clients.

How do I know how much I should give to someone with whom I'm negotiating?

That's a tough question without knowing more context, but what I can say is that its not hard to think about what you are getting and what they are getting.

The most comment assets to balance are time and money related. For instance, one partner may need to put in much more time, so they should get more of the revenue. If someone is doing 20% of the work, they deserve only 20% of the revenue. If they are doing 80%, they deserve 80% of the revenue.

Do you get these things in contract?

Not until we've proven the business model will work. There are a number of reasons for this including that real contracts can take months to review and cost thousands of dollars to have lawyers review them.

However, I do get our agreement in writing 100% of the time. (Email is preferred but text messages work, too.)

I do this because people forget the details in a few weeks or months, and also because anything written down is technically a contract. Especially if you require the other person to respond back with "Agree," which I always do.

The only time I'll do a real contract early on is when the other partner requires it or when the project is really big and there is a major investing being laid out early (in either time or money) by either party.

Have you ever had a partnership go bad?

Yes. In fact, when you deal with people who don't know what they are doing, it happens more than 50% of the time. Make sure your agreement is written down and that you have a conversation about what you want your break-up to look like because no business partnership lasts a lifetime.

That is a real conversation I have early on with every one of my partners. Over your lifetime, you might have one or two partnerships that last more than a few years. Markets change, opportunities change, goals change, and partners eventually part ways so having a general understanding of what to expect from each other is always helpful.

Now, this don't mean the break-up will happen as expected because the reality is that most business break-ups happen because of a conflict of some sort. It's at this time when you find out someone's real character and maturity. I've had partners look me in the eye early on and say, "James, I promise you I would never leave this partnership in a negative way; I'm just not that type of person" and then that same person breaks up our partnership by having only their lawyer talk to me because that person is not good with handling conflict and he just didn't want to face the music.

People get funny and weird when the pressure is on, so be aware that the break-up is not likely to go as planned, but I can tell you that talking about it early on has helped a ton and saved me tens of thousands of dollars.

Have you ever been out-leveraged in a deal?

Yes. All the time, in fact. But those are deals where my goal isn't short-term, and I'm usually trying to prove myself to someone or build long-term equity and trust with them, so I might allow them to get the bigger portion of gains. Letting someone else have the advantage in leverage is a good business strategy if you're in control (meaning you're aware it's happening, and it's calculated on your side).

When you get screwed is when you're not aware that you're getting out-leveraged—or worse, you are aware of it, and your personality makes you a yes man or someone who just gives in and says, "Yeah that's fine; I'm not worried about those minor details."

The devil is always in those details, so never think that not talking through the minor details and getting a collective understanding of the leverage in the deal is a waste of time.

Shouldn't you always work then with someone who's not going to take advantage of you?

In a perfect world, yes, but the reality is no. Probably 80% of my best deals of all time are with people who, if they had a chance to take a little bit of an advantage of me, they would. If you let them take advantage of you, it's not personal, so don't take it that way. You're letting them, and "it's just business."

THE ULTIMATE LEVER

James, you talk about the most leverage being in social media and video right now, but you also talk about money being the ultimate lever. Can you explain?

Social media and video are the best "technologies" to leverage. Money, however, is your number one asset to leverage.

I say money (over time) because if you make money, you can create free time and automations so you have more time. But I know a ton of entrepreneurs who are amazing at leveraging their time, but they are broke (they just don't make enough money).

I've found in life that money is the most universal tool you'll never have in your tool belt. It's like having a tool that can change your tire, fix your broken window in your house, and wash your dishes—all at the same time.

Nothing like that really exists, but money can easily enable all those things to happen without you even knowing they are going on.

I'm not encouraging people to serve money or live their life just for money, but I do think money can serve you and serve you very well.

SYSTEMS OF LEVERAGE

James, how do I start to create more leverage in my life and business?

I wish I had time to go into it all, but that would take me months to explain. And realistically, its different for people based on their skillsets and passions.

But I can say this: You can't create proper leverage without knowing "systems of leverage."

Yes, even to max-out on leverage in your life and business, you need to "leverage" how leverage works. I've discovered many systems to leverage and taught literally tens of thousands how to max-out on leverage in their life.

James, can you give an example of how to max-out on leverage of my network?

Sure. I've probably helped a thousand people make their first six figures of residual income doing this.

1. List all the VIP type of people you know. Go through your phone contact list, your emails, your social media, etc and list out ten to one-hundred people. Chet Holmes called this "The Dream 100" in his book *The Ultimate Sales Machine*, but I've learned to execute on this list 10x better than he suggests.

2. Next to each name, write out exactly what this person wants. Not what they need, not what they do, it has to be what they ultimately WANT right now. If you don't know, pick up the phone and call them or message them on social media.

3. Step back from that list and see if there are matches. Does someone on that list want to meet someone else on that list. Inevitably, there will be matches.

4. Call or PM the person who know the most and ask them, "Would you like to meet someone who [what they ultimately

want]? Want me to get you connected?" Get their agreement, then ask them if they'll pay you 10% of any business done between them and your contact. Get your deal written down in email or some form of writing so you have a record of it.

5. Call or PM the other person and say, "Hey, someone who [what this person ultimately wants] wants to talk to you. Want me to connect you two?" You can also ask this person for 10%, too!

6. Connect the two parties and then follow up each month to see how much is billed between them. Do this for life, and if needed, get an accountant involved who matches up commissions with their accountant so you're always getting paid.

Do this five hours every day for six months, and I promise you'll be making six figures.

NEXT STEP ON CREATING LEVERAGE

James, can you help me create this type of leverage and income?

I'm not sure, it completely depends on how dedicated you are to become a real entrepreneur and if you are willing to put in the work to make it happen.

But if you're willing and have the passion and drive, I have hundreds of systems like this, and I'll get you matched up with the right system and help you crush it.

James, does this work if I have an existing business and just want to make a few more million or a few ten million or more?

Absolutely. I started off doing this myself before starting to work with solopreneurs, so yes, it works, and it works better for companies who already have revenue.

James, how do I follow up with you?

Book a complimentary strategy meeting with me or one of my Elite Team Members here and let's see if you're ready to achieve maximum leverage.

ABOUT JAMES SMILEY

James has been recognized as one of the most innovative and in-demand entrepreneurs under 40. He has led $0 to $20M growth for two different companies, been a part of a Silicon Valley SaaS IPO, and consulted for 3 of the Fortune 10.

James has been the behind-the-scenes paid advisor to over 560 executives and entrepreneurs. His primary specialty is helping entrepreneurs with rapid revenue acceleration by leveraging online automation and his proprietary digital marketing systems.

James has published 8 books, recorded over 10,000+ videos and podcasts, trained over 12,000 B2B sales reps, delivered 600+ speeches, and sold over $210M before the age of 35.

He played some college football and is a former ESPN Bassmaster pro angler and fished in the Bassmaster National Championship.

info@jamessmiley.org
jamessmiley.org/freeusb

NOTES

NOTES

NOTES

MASTERING INFLUENCE AND INCOME ONLINE

by Steve Larsen

I n college, my favorite spot to study, build funnels, and learn marketing was in the restricted box office seats in the basketball stadium on campus. Since the box seats weren't allowed and the doors were always locked, I'd act like I was on my phone in front of the box seat windows, up in the stands. As soon as the security guys would turn their heads, I'd throw my bag in and climb up through the window. It was quiet up there, had fast Internet, and I could stay way past building close. I did that for almost a year and a half.

I had been spending a huge amount of time studying Internet gurus, and it was the perfect set up for my geek out sessions. Was it kinda lonely? A bit. But it was also a massive accelerator for me.

Since we didn't have money for another car, I'd ride my bike back and forth each day to campus. In some ways, I miss that. I remember riding back to our little apartment one beautiful summer day. I was mentally beating myself up with phrases like, *Why am I still poor*, *What's wrong with you, Steve; why isn't this working yet*, and *I know what I'd do in this scenario and that scenario, but how come I still have zero cash?* By then, I'd been going at this Internet marketing game for a couple years but all I had to show for it was lost money and lost pride.

Now, I don't know why, but suddenly this huge epiphany hit me rather abruptly. *Marketing isn't selling. Selling isn't marketing.* Hmm... As a marketing student in college, the phrase even felt a little weird coming out of me. I knew it was truth, but it felt like yet another shot to my pride because I had been doing door-to-door sales and telemarketing with the explicit intent to learn sales. And I wasn't bad at it either. But now, what I needed most was to learn marketing. So before moving on, what's the difference between the two?

As stated by Joe Polish, sales is what happens face to face with a prospective customer, but marketing is how you get them *to* your face. Whoa! Said another way, <u>marketing is changing someone's beliefs with the intent to sell.</u>

I'm convinced that the Internet is most ripe and gold-filled for those who study marketing above sales. I'm also convinced that long-term influence and income online has everything to do with marketing and not sales.

This isn't to downplay the importance of sales. Sales makes the world and my business go 'round, but hear my point. With so many distractions and ads on the Internet today, it's wise to be an expert in getting people "to your face."

Frankly, if I were asked to write a chapter about influence and income online four years ago, I would've just laughed in disbelief. I'm floored by everything that's happened to my life in such a short amount of time.

Today, you may currently be a big influencer, or you may be completely brand new. For me, though, four years ago I was as green as they come. It's not like I started without an email list. I had no list. No one knew who I was. Yet oddly enough, once I began a deep study of what marketing really was, my influence and income grew in tandem.

Looking back, though, it's clear that influence and income are tied. Especially online. One doesn't really grow without the other. The more income I've had, the more money I've dumped back into <u>gaining more influence</u>. And the more influence I've had, the faster the money has dropped in.

I don't believe the sexy mirage of being an introverted rich person. Hiding behind a computer screen is not possible anymore. Maybe it was five years ago, but not anymore. It's time to become the "attractive character" of your business. It's time to learn to be the one standing and delivering.

The good news, especially if you don't have a following yet, is that this whole game is a formula, meaning *it can be learned*. It's not hard, but it's also not taught, which makes these skills truly rare.

This is the purpose for why I'm writing right now, to expose the formula that your personal character needs to be an online success.

While I can't go into great depth here, I do want to cover several specific points, which when applied, will bring you influence *and* income online. Again, my goal through these points is to paint a picture of the marketing formula that your own attractive character needs. I'm talking about the "two comma club" layout for *you*, not your business. I treat the marketing for each very differently. Deal? Let me explain.

First, your business competes on strengths in the marketplace. It's a game where the strongest gets paid. It's an active bloody war of who has the best product, who delivers the most results, and who keeps the market the happiest.

Second, your personal, attractive character does not compete in that way. While your business competes on strengths, it's imperative to understand that your personal attractive character competes on differences. Why? Someone will always be a stronger speaker than I am, a faster writer, or personally better at this or that, but only I can compete with my differences. There's only one me.

New entrepreneurs get their personal attractive character chewed up and spit out when they try to compete on strengths. It's futile. Instead, treat your business strategy and your attractive character strategy differently.

Just know there's a big difference because, for the remainder of this chapter, I'm not going talk about the marketing for your business. We're talking about the marketing for *you!*

As I've taught these concepts to thousands of entrepreneurs now, I've found that the principle of the "attractive character" is the most glossed over topic of any category. That's a tragedy because it's one of the fast tracks to influence *and* income.

I'm a believer that competence equals confidence, and if I don't feel confident enough, I usually just don't know enough. For fear, you may approach the principle of the "attractive character" without confidence. Let me give three axioms to show you how to pull off this beast of a principle.

Note that these obviously don't make a complete list but are most often the very points that get people to take action when I'm teaching this principle on stages.

AXIOM ONE - STORY AMPLIFIES VALUE

"Talk" with me for a minute here. As I write this chapter, I have an American flag to my right, hanging on the wall. Just out of curiosity, what do you think the retail value of that flag is? A quick Google search just told me that I can buy one for $23.14.

Please pay attention to one of the most important lessons I can hand off here, and let me tell you about the flag on my wall.

After I got my Eagle Scout Award (thanks to my mom, ha) a U.S. Senator was told to hang that very flag on my wall on the White House for me specifically. So, he did and this flag was flown on the White House. I have a personal certificate to prove it.

That being said, the first one to send me $23.14 can take it right off of my wall. Come on down, or I'll just ship it to you.

Wait, why don't you believe me? What just happened? Something just happened to the value of that flag. Why wouldn't I part with it for $23.14 even though Google already said that's what the flag is probably worth.

Because of the story. Because story amplifies value! Because story changes and gives context to facts. Was there already an inherent value in that flag? Yes! Not only did Google say it costs $23.14 retail, but I'm guessing the actual manufacturing and material costs were maybe a dollar or two.

Notice that it's the *value* of the flag that just went way up because of the story. Price and value are not the same thing, which makes me never want to give that flag away. The *price* of $23.14 or any amount of money feels like an insult to me because the story makes the *value* so high.

"Steve, what does this have to do with my attractive character?"

Okay, get how cool this is! After sitting next to Russell Brunson for two years as his Lead Funnel Builder at ClickFunnels, and after seeing tens of thousands of entrepreneur's funnels, I'm going to drop a big 'ol secret weapon on you. It's a pattern I started seeing, and it became very apparent to me. This is such a big deal that it acts as an extra layer of security for you and your business and should inspire you to just move forward as an influencer with income. Here's the pattern.

After personally seeing over 1,000 Internet entrepreneur's offers and funnels in just the last three years alone (most of whom were students of mine), I've learned that the vast majority of any problems someone faces when selling their products have little to do with the product itself.

Ironically, it became more and more apparent that the ones who were drenched in income certainly did have great products, but there was a stronger force at play. I'm hoping that the lesson I'm about to teach you should help you understand that your Internet success is not dependent on you having an outstanding product. Have I set the stage long enough? Are you writhing in anticipation? Here it is.

Virtually all issues have to do with the marketer's inability to do just that—market. The knee jerk mistake a new Internet entrepreneur tends to believe is that their income and success will be based on how good their product is. Just so we're clear, that belief is complete garbage!

While the product matters greatly and hopefully over-delivers on the promised value, influence and income is hinged on the entrepreneur's abilities to tell story and produce content. That's it. Only there do you gain a base-following large and loyal enough to practically ensure the success of any product you release in the future.

This reminds me of something Dan Kennedy said: "The only asset that can be kept safe from every threat and made to appreciate in value year after year is the relationship you have with your customers." And you do this through storytelling.

My big fear when I say this to people is that they think of books like *Goodnight Moon* and *The Cat In The Hat*. Hear me out.

Storytelling and content producing are the highest leverage skills any entrepreneur could gain, and is in reality, the only real asset you possess. When my students are struggling to sell, the extreme vast majority of the time the problem isn't their offer, funnel, or even their products. This is huge. Failure to sell is usually not an offer problem, it's a storytelling problem.

Want influence and income? Get scary amazing at telling stories that sell.

AXIOM TWO - CONSTRAINTS ARE CATALYSTS

ClickFunnels has this event called Funnel Hacking Live. I didn't make it to the first Funnel Hacking Live event because our first daughter was due around the same time and missing the birth was obviously not an option.

Plus, we didn't have the cash for me to go to something like that, anyway. We were living on student loans. Our first year of marriage we "made" $18k total in loans.

What was great about that is it gave me time to figure out how to get there the following year.

name drop

"Okay", I told myself. "Robert Kiyosaki says that poor people say they can't afford something, while rich people ask how they can afford something. So, how am I going to do this?"

I had actually been an early adopter of the ClickFunnels software and knew how to build funnels, but I was doing them for free *a lot* just to practice. (There was probably a little fear to charge money running through my head too.)

All I wanted to figure out was how to get to Funnel Hacking Live 2016, and I had one year to figure it out. So, I started building funnels for people without any expectation for money. Instead, I told them I'd like to build a funnel in exchange for a few hotel nights or a two-way plane ticket or a Funnel Hacking Live 2016 ticket.

Keep in mind that this was in the middle of college, the Army, a new baby, being married, debts, etc. I was extremely busy. I'd only sleep a few hours each night so I could study funnels and build funnels almost every night. It was funnels, funnels, funnels. Most people had no idea what I was doing, and many thought I was selling kitchen funnels—ha.

I hustled like an animal, though. I *wanted* to get to that event. I *needed* to be in the room. I just knew that if I could get in the room that my life would change somehow. I couldn't explain it.

So, I kept building funnels and saying yes to whatever else the client wanted me to do, which I usually had no clue how to do but also figured it out after a few hours of YouTube videos.

A very interesting thing happened, though. By the time I actually got to Funnel Hacking Live a year later and bootstrapped my entire way, I had read pretty much every ClickFunnels Support Doc they had. I had also written into their Support almost twice, every day, for a full year. They knew who I was!

So, when I checked into the event table for my ticket, I also ended up getting a job offer for ClickFunnels. Then, another four offers from different ClickFunnels leaders throughout the remainder of the event. Five job offers!

"Steve, you're talking about yourself a lot!" I know. Hear me when I say this: I am thoroughly convinced to my very bones that I would *never* have worked for ClickFunnels, or especially been Russell Brunson's right-hand funnel builder, if I *did* have the money to get to that Funnel Hacking Live event. Make sense? There's no way! I wouldn't have been prepared enough or had enough experience to even talk about.

The fact that I did not have cash made me do, learn, and experience things in a way that I would not have done otherwise. This pattern has happened multiple times in my life in massive ways.

There's a coin that sits on my desk with one of my favorite quotes on it that says, ("The Obstacle Is The Way. The Impediment To Action Advances Action. What Stands In The Way Becomes The Way.")

So, what does this have to do with influence and income online? *"Freakin' everything"* is the full and correct technical answer. It has to do with everything in entrepreneurship.

Look, most of the time, I find that people actually *do* know what they need to do next to grow their business but are just trying to get the courage to act. I totally get it.

As this relates to your attractive character, if you have an obstacle in your way, then I'm very excited for you. I hope its gigantic and completely overwhelming. I want you to be overwhelmed like you never have been because you know your next step in the path.

Not all stress is bad. There's eustress, as in euphoria. It's defined as, "moderate or normal psychological stress interpreted as being beneficial for the experiencer." Then there's distress, as in destructive stress. Do not confuse the two.

The most influential people in my life and my business have always gone through at least one massive form of eustress. But culturally, we dismiss the growth opportunity as distress. Don't believe it.

If you want to influence people, you will lean into your own obstacles. Hard! The story you create and experience while overcoming your own obstacles is like gasoline on the fire of your attractive character.

The true, real, and raw stories of you overcoming your own obstacles are gifts to others. They're one of the most paramount forms influencing others that you'll ever gain.

So, I say, lean in!

What's wrong with you is really your superpower and a magnet to a loyal following online. That's not a joke. I mean all of what's "wrong" with you.

Have some fear right now? Maybe dyslexia? A speech impediment or learning disability? Feel like you're not perfect or a fit enough for the Internet game? As a friend, let me tell you that while those fears feel convincing and logical, they're garbage.

I got the Nicest Kid Award in my graduating class of 600 people in high school. It shocked me. It almost offended me. I wasn't nice. I was shy! I had very little confidence. I think I got it because it took me quite a while to warm up to the idea of talking around people. I was totally a follower but the fearful kind.

I hated seeing an adult coming down the hall toward me. I'd get nervous sometimes and just start walking the other way. That's also not a joke. Once I became self-aware of it, I decided to lean into the constraint.

I guarantee that someone reading this right now has felt or been through the same. The fact that I tell those stories invigorates and inspires people to overcome the same. Income follows, and everyone wins.

A counselor told me I had a lot of ADHD symptoms. Yeah, so? While at first I was afraid of having those kind of letters after my name, it's how I can push so hard.

What's "wrong" with you is your superpower and also the path for you to lean into. Again, why am I writing about this in this book? Please see how this is everything in being influential.

I was texting one of my coaches a few months ago (I have several coaches for several topics who push me, and I like to keep them nearby so they can keep me in check).

I had just gone through a particularly hard week of producing for my business and was feeling a combination of stress, fear, and a bit of anxiety over the next wave of crazy action we were planning on. I was trying to cope.

This is exactly what I texted one of my coaches, Alex Charfen: "Who knew the psychological junk of this game would be so freakin' hard. The money part is ironically the easier of the two. I'd never have guessed this." To which he replied, "Welcome to the real world of entrepreneurship. This is where the rubber meets the road and exactly why so many people struggle and remain small…"

Ladies and gentlemen, any pursuit toward influence and income will be barraged by the enemies both outside and inside of your head. The question isn't whether or not you'll get a little uncomfortable or afraid in this journey. The question is what you will do once it starts so it doesn't derail you.

As Susan Jeffers says, "Feel the fear, and do it anyway." Your experiences and obstacles become influential powerhouses down the road. Because of that, don't be afraid to live out your own journey with hope in your eyes. (You could currently be living the story that shapes and changes someone's entire life and the generations behind it very soon.)

AXIOM THREE - PUBLISH OR DIE

About two years after we were married, I enlisted in the Army. It's something I wanted to do, plus the insurance was great, and the small amount of money each month kept us alive.

After returning from Basic, I joined the ROTC to become an officer. One semester, I remember doing endless hours of sprints around the track. The smell of sweat on the track in the hot sun is still burned in my memory (ugh… sprint day).

One day, as I ran by my phone sitting on the side of the track, I saw a notification that Russell Brunson had just started a Periscope, which I always enjoyed.

I quickly swiped my phone open and heard some massively devastating instructions from him. "Make sure you start publishing a lot!" Crap. Seriously?

This was devastating because I treated what he said like orders, which meant I had to do it. (Which is another reason I'm convinced everything awesome has happened so quickly in the last four years.) His instructions were to pick some platform I liked, like a blog, podcast, video, etc., and stay consistent with it.

My mind was spinning with objections to the idea of publishing. They were the more deeply seated reasons that I didn't want to listen to him.

"I'm not qualified to do something like publish. Who would listen anyway? I don't have a following at all. What would I say? Will I run out of things to say? Am I enough of an expert to do this? Will people think I'm a fraud? *Am* I a fraud?"

I know the standard objections so well because they were also mine *and* they're also the same ones everyone else gives me when I tell them to start publishing.

Let's get over those fear right now. First off, no, those are not rational fears and you should learn to call yourself on your own b.s.

Secondly, not to get all "Army" on you, but the easiest and most basic way to trip up an enemy is to mess with their communications. Or just stop communicating all together. Get it? Scaling and growing a successful business (or any organization) requires more communication on your part.

If you do not publish, no one knows you or your products even exist. Publishing is one of the most basic, fundamental vehicles of marketing. It is not an option. It *is* marketing. It *is* influence, and with time, it practically guarantees income online. You're dead in the water if you opt out of publishing.

So, whether it's a matter of figuring out your first steps or merely getting tough with yourself—publish! The Internet is show business. But here's a few more loving reasons why you need to publish.

A big false belief I had about publishing was that I thought I already needed to be an expert before I started. False. False. False. In fact, waiting to publish until you're a hot shot is a big handicap because you're far less believable when you've already made it.

By the time I got hired to be Russell Brunson's funnel building assistant, I had heard him tell me to start publishing several times. Reluctantly, I began. If you listen to the first twenty episodes of Sales

Funnel Radio, you'll hear the awkwardness. The content was good, but delivery was terrible.

Yet, something happened around episode thirty. It was something Russell kept telling me would happen, but it was also something he said he couldn't teach me. I had to learn it by experience. I found my "voice." Then, my followers, influence, and income went up. You'll do the same if you trust the process.

Around episode eighty, I again felt myself bring in far more polarity. And again, my followers, influence, and income went up.

One day, I walked into Russell's office and said, "Dude, I just listened to the first few episodes of my podcast and they were terrible. I think I'm going delete them." He whipped around and practically yelled (something he doesn't do), "Noooo! That's how they know you were human once! Keep 'em!"

Okay. Allow me to get a little passionate here. If there's any pain relief and sincere advice I can hand you while you begin publishing, it's this: You need to understand the power of becoming the expert in front of your audience.

Beginning while you're not a pro yet is a huge upper hand. It's not that you just stack the deck in your favor, you take the other guru's card completely. It lets you be more followable and believable. Only then, will they truly cheer for your successes *with you,* and they'll feel your pains *with you* as they watch your journey to the top.

You want influence and income but don't know what to talk about? Get raw. Expose your flaws. They make the best stories and headlines. I'm not telling you to be all mopey and self-defeating. That's annoying. But your experiences are unique to you and a catalyst for your following. In the end, you need to "buy" the customer somehow, and if you don't have cash for ads, then plan on spending some time to "buy" them instead. Your flaws, quirks, and differences are exceptional at doing this.

Are you nervous in the moment? Then say it to your audience. Don't like suits? Then don't wear one. Have a favorite hobby? Let your audience know. Have a strong opinion on a public matter? Oh, baby! Get ready for followers and some haters, which is perfect.

Don't know what to say? I didn't either for a long time. Here's an easy fix. Pick a big worthy goal and make it your mission publicly.

everyday is an opportunity to P.S.
& you're only one PSA

Connect with your audience over it. Then, simply document your journey towards hitting the goal. Both good and bad, as it's happening. That's literally how Sales Funnel Radio happens as I "call my shot" right in my intro. It ruffles feathers and bands my listeners together at the same time.

This simple strategy keeps you from waiting to begin because you feel like you're not a professional yet. That's crap and a lie from Hollywood. You're good at something. I truly thought I couldn't start this game because I didn't own a briefcase. I know it sounds stupid, and it was. But what's holding you back from publishing? It's probably stupid, too.

This next lesson comes right from the heart. The Internet game isn't a game of changing who you are for the sake of an audience. You'll fail. People smell fake. This game is a beautiful, liberating game where you get to be you, louder! There's no other business that lets you do this.

I have massive eyeballs. I know it. So, I say it. Sometimes I stutter still, even on stage. Who cares. I love my rock, trap, and a little rap music. Yeah? I'm a 30-year-old that longboards barefoot with massive headphones on. Yep. The big secret is that I repel as many people as I attract. Perfect!

There's a facade of "professionalism" that we need to have to be successful, especially online (thanks LinkedIn, Pinterest, and college classes). Maybe in the age of the baby boomers that was true, but that door is closed. It's time for you to become a character and get followable with the weird quirks you have as storylines.

Welcome to the most freakin' awesome game in the world, and welcome to loving what you do. I absolutely love what I do, but don't tell me I'm lucky. I've worked hard to get it, and you can too.

I hope this has been helpful to you. Not to sound dumb, but to have a big influence and income you must be influencing people. I don't know how you can do that without learning to tell awesome stories, using your obstacles as headlines, and publishing frequently about them.

Again, as a reminder, the three axioms fit together. Good storytelling is the sign of a true marketer and constraints aren't actually constraints when you lean into and publish about how you overcame them. It's a very simple and incredibly effective formula. The consistent execution of these three axioms will drastically increase your influence and income, online or offline.

A final word of caution. Learning to tell, create, and publish stories is married to the powers of persuasion. Please be ethical in how you influence the very real lives and opinions of others. You are literally learning to change the frames that someone sees the world and their personal beliefs. It's the closest thing to real mind control that exists. It's also one of the reasons I both love what I do but feel a solemn mantle at the same time.

Hopefully, this short chapter calmed fears and painted a picture for you about the worthy pursuit of influence and income, especially as it pertains to your attractive character. Just do it.

As Charles Bukowski said, "If you can fill the unforgiving minute, the sixty seconds worth of distance run, yours is the earth and everything that's in it. If you're going to try, go all the way. ...Otherwise, don't even start. ...And it will be better than anything else you can imagine."

ABOUT STEVE LARSEN

For two years, Steve Larsen was the Lead Funnel Builder at ClickFunnels for Russell Brunson and put over 500 sales funnels under his belt (but honestly lost track a while ago).

Eventually, he left ClickFunnels as an employee to get his own Two Comma Club Award, and his business crossed $1 million only 13 months later. His podcast Sales Funnel Radio was created to share best practices and teach the finer points of marketing, offer creation, and "funnelology."

Steve's approach to offers is so attractive that fans body-check their own grandmas just to buy. Long walks on the beach aren't his thing, but he loves slappin' five.

support@stevejlarsen.zohodesk.com
stevejlarsen.com

NOTES

NOTES

THE GAME OF SOCIAL MEDIA

by Josh Forti

At any point in history, there is always a major opportunity that can be capitalized upon, one that will make many people rich and create entire industries around it. It is easy to assume that not everyone has access to these opportunities and that they are "only for people with money or connections." And, in some cases in history, that might have been the case.

But that is not the case with today's opportunity. In fact, if ever there were a time in the history of mankind where there was an opportunity that was equally available to everyone, now is that time.

That opportunity is social media.

What social media brings to the table is unlike any other opportunity ever before in the history of the human race. And if your goal is to master influence and income, welcome to the future.

Anyone—regardless of age, race, body type, social status, etc.—can now build a mass following, create unlimited income, and deliver their message to the masses using social media.

I know this to be true because my career is proof of that. In fact, just three years ago, I didn't have an Instagram account. I had less than two hundred friends on Facebook, and I was milking goats and bailing hay on a little farm in northeastern Indiana.

Fast-forward to today where I've mastered the art of utilizing social media to deliver my message to millions. This has put me on stage in front of thousands, landed me business deals with major brands and influencers like Grant Cardone, and allowed me to work with hundreds of entrepreneurs to increase their influence, audience, and income, all before the age of 25.

The question I always get asked is, "How?"

This chapter will give you the blueprint of understanding the game of social media. Yes, it is a game. Don't let anyone tell you otherwise.

Understand how the game works, and you can literally set any income and influence level you want.

Don't understand that game, and you will be mindlessly posting words on a page and hoping someone comes along and is bored enough to listen to you.

Let me start by saying that I didn't write this chapter to entertain you, to make you feel good, or to brag about my success.

This chapter is designed with one thing in mind—to show you how to build a following on social media that loves your message and pays you for your advice.

Social media is here, and it is here to stay. It continues to fundamentally change the way we do business, build influence, and have an impact on the world today.

But what you're trying to figure out is how.

How do I increase my income and influence using social media? You know it is possible, but you don't know how.

Over the course of the past several years of my career, I have studied countless successful influencers and looked for the commonalities they all have. I then took that information and applied it to my own brand to see what worked and what didn't.

Growing influence and income on any social media, regardless of the platform, industry, or type of business you are trying to build, comes down to three core elements.

Let's dive in.

ELEMENT #1: A CLEARLY DEFINED, SIMPLY STATED MESSAGE

First, notice I didn't just say "a message."

Having a message, whatever that may be, is great. But if people can't understand your message, or don't know what your message is, you won't get very far.

Your core message idea does not have to be, and should not be, complex. It simply has to be clearly defined and phrased in a way that people can understand it.

Look at Donald Trump, for example. (Put all politics aside, it doesn't matter whether you like him or not, but look at what he did.)

While running for president, he had one very clear message: Make America Great Again.

Whether or not you liked him or knew about his policies or how he planned to accomplish his message, you knew what it was.

And by the end of his campaign, the words "Make America Great Again" were like an extension of the name Donald Trump.

Now, you may be wondering what this has to do with social media. It has everything to do with it.

When you are trying to build a following online and master the game of social media, step one—before you do anything else—you have to identify and clearly state what your message is, and you need to do it in the simplest, most clearly defined way possible.

There are over three billion people on social media today. In order for you to set yourself apart, and to get people to follow you, your audience has to know what you're about. What is the core message or idea that you stand for?

When I first got into the social media game, I didn't know what I was doing, but I realized that every successful person I followed had a message or theme they stood by. Whether it was Russell Brunson with "You're just one funnel away," or Grant Cardone with "10X" and "Who's got my money," when I heard their names, I knew what they were about. So, I became the Instagram guy. My message was simple. "Grow fast on Instagram the right way." When people heard my name, they thought Instagram. As I have grown, that message has become more, turning into "social media," but my core audience still knows me as "the Instagram guy."

I cannot stress this enough. You need to know your message and how to effectively communicate that message to your audience.

Here are three tips for crafting your message.

#1. Be simple. The person who says it the simplest wins.

#2. Be relatable. People need to be able to own it as their own.

#3. Be consistent. Whatever you decide your message is, everything you do should point back to it.

When someone hears your name, they should immediately associate it with whatever your message is about.

(Russell Brunson - Funnels. Grant Cardone - Money. Josh Forti - Social Media.)

ELEMENT #2: GET ATTENTION

Social Media is a game of attention. That. Is. It.

The algorithms that decide what gets shown to who are all based on attention. The more engagement (attention) you get on your content, the more people see it. This is true on every platform. Don't over-complicate how social media works. It is just a game of who can get the most engagement. It is why click bait still works and gets massive views. You need to do whatever it takes to get attention. So many people miss this.

Say what you want about the Kardashians, Kanye West, or Donald Trump, they've mastered this. The attention is always on them. Negative attention or engagement on your content is not a bad thing. It means you stand for something. As long as your content is in alignment with your message, there is no such thing as bad publicity.

Throughout my career in social media, whether it was growing millions on Instagram, building one of the fastest growing social media-related Facebook groups on the planet, or watching my friends destroy their competition on YouTube, there were three main strategies used to master attention. Those of us who used them won almost every single time.

STEP #1: BE POLARIZING/BOLD/CONTROVERSIAL

People hate boring and neutral. Content that is neutral and that everyone agrees with gets the least engagement and makes the least sales. You want the attention on you, and you want people to fall in love with your message. In order to get that, you need to stand for something.

When I first started positioning myself as an influencer and expert in my industry, I started making statements that were bold, new, and projections of the future. I was in the Instagram world, and I would make statements about how Instagram was going to be the next big platform (even when it was small) and showed people ways that I was dominating Instagram growth. I started disagreeing with other Instagram "experts" in my niche who I thought were doing Instagram growth the wrong way. I was very blunt about it yet still remained respectful.

You need to be bold and not be afraid to make polarizing or controversial statements about what you stand for. Maintain absolute certainty in your message. It is okay for people to disagree with you. In fact, it is encouraged. Lots of people disagreed with me at the beginning, and thought I was a little crazy. But, it increased my engagement and solidified my status as a thought leader and influencer in my industry. As time went on, I maintained certainty in my message, proved my concepts, and as a result, the attention stayed on me. Mainstream doesn't sell. Polarity and bold statements do.

STEP #2: BE PROLIFIC AND CONSISTENT

You need to produce A LOT of content. Social media is a content-driven world. Creating and publishing content daily is a must. Back when I was managing multiple million followers on Instagram, we were publishing up to six pieces of content per day per account. The result? A lot of people saw a lot of my content, which resulted in millions of followers. Think of social media as a huge pile of cards.

Every piece of content on social media is a card, and your ideal audience only gets to see the cards (content) toward the top of the pile. There are only two ways to get to the top. The first is to be the latest person to post content, thereby being at the top of the pile until someone else comes along and puts their card on top of yours. The second is to get lots of people to read your card (engagement), thus keeping it on the top of the pile.

However, for every card you put on the pile, it builds a bigger and bigger platform because you have more cards, so your cards take longer to be pushed down because more and more people want to see your stuff. The more content you put out, the more you get seen.

If you are publishing once a week, and your competition is publishing twice a day, your competition is going to grow 30 to 50 times faster than you are because of the combination of them having more cards (content) and the compound effect of engagement/the cards working together. If you want to compete, you have to publish more. This is true regardless of the platform.

There is almost no such thing as too much content. It is important to note that your content actually needs to be good, it needs to be related to your message, and it needs to consistently present new ideas as times goes on to keep your audience engaged and their eyes on you. If your content isn't good, then it doesn't matter how much of it you put out.

I understood this concept better than almost all of my competition. I posted content around the clock, all hours of the day, to capitalize on all time zones and audiences worldwide.

STEP #3: GO WHERE THE ATTENTION IS

It amazes me how many people look at me with that "deer in the headlights" look when I say this. Think of it this way—there are people all over the world, but how much more effective is a billboard in Time Square in New York City than it is in the middle of a small town with 500 people in it? Way more effective. Why? Because people are there. That is where the attention is. The same thing is true on social media.

When I first started growing my audience online, I was a nobody without any followers. Most people just put content out there and hope the followers come. What they don't realize is that most of the time they are putting their content on a billboard in the middle of a small town instead of putting it in Times Square.

I realized this and understood that if I wanted to get more attention on me, I had to go where the attention was. (It is much easier to go to the attention in the beginning than it is to bring the attention to you.) I did that by figuring out where the audience that I wanted to attract hung out. I found and got in/on Facebook groups, podcasts, live stream interviews, shout-outs from big pages that had my ideal audience, etc. I figured out where the attention was and put my content there.

Social media is packed full of what I call "engagement pockets," small pockets of people that are all very interactive with whatever it is they are following. Find the engagement pockets in your industry, capitalize on them, and watch your numbers soar.

I cannot stress to you enough that these principles are true regardless of the platform you are on. Platforms change, little tricks on how to get more views change, but these fundamentals are true across the board. Focus on getting the attention on you.

ELEMENT #3. KEEP, DUPLICATE AND DIVERSIFY ATTENTION

Once you have attention on one platform, it is crucially important for the longevity of your brand that you keep that attention.

Attention, especially in today's society, doesn't last very long, so maintaining that attention is actually much more complex than "just posting a lot of good content."

There are three important parts of keeping your audience's attention for long periods of time.

#1. STORYLINE/STORY TELLING

If you want to keep people engaged, give them a story. And I don't mean a long post with some good copy or a two-hour webinar where you keep them engaged the whole time.

I mean that your brand, your message, and who you are should tell a story like something new and exciting that you are working on, a new idea that you are presenting, and the suspense of what is next. The hero's journey, which is what every major film and storyline is based off of, is a phenomenal concept to study. Integrating that formula into your brand will keep you in the front of your audience's mind.

#2. CROSS PROMOTION ON PLATFORMS

Once you grow an audience, do not stay on one platform. Not only do you set yourself up for disaster if something were to happen to your account, but you are also limiting the amount of time your followers can see you and consume your content.

The average person has to see an offer six to eight times before they consider buying something. That same principle is true on social media. Your average follower has to consume a certain number of pieces of your content to become a true fan. That number varies for each audience, but it is almost impossible to be a dominant player or trusted thought leader if your audience is only following you on one platform.

You will typically have one dominant platform, the one where you are most well-known or get your start on, but your true fans, your buyers, and the ones who will promote you to their friends, are the ones who follow you everywhere. So you need to be everywhere.

Integrate different parts/angles of your story on different platforms so your audience is drawn from one platform to the next. This will keep them engaged long-term, allow them to get to know you better, and make them fall further into your brand and way of thinking.

Instagram, Facebook, YouTube, and an email list are the big four, but there are countless other platforms you can capitalize on such as Twitter, Snapchat, podcasts, a blog, Pinterest, Twitch, etc. Cross promotion/omnipresence is the key to long-term success. Don't just sit on one platform.

STEP #3. PROVIDE VALUE THAT BRINGS A DESIRED RESULT

It is important to realize that people follow, engage with, and buy from you for one reason—what you can do for them. Regardless of what you think, and no matter how nice of a person you are, people don't follow you because you are nice or because they are nice. They are in this for themselves. That isn't a bad thing. In fact, when you capitalize upon that, it actually makes your audience more loyal.

Providing tools, formulas, ideas, products, or resources that provide a desired result for your audience is the surest way to get your audience to never leave you. If you can change their life for the better, and get them something they want, it's like they have a moral obligation to follow you. And it works.

Having both free and paid resources for them to consume and taking them through the value ladder (see *Dotcom Secrets* by Russell Brunson) will indoctrinate your audience into your way of thinking and keep them coming back for more, every time.

Phew. I know that was a lot of information packed into a short chapter! You are probably feeling like you just learned more from this chapter than you would have from an entire college degree. (Believe me, you did.) I understand that. The concepts that I laid out in this chapter took me several years and thousands of hours of testing and application to master. I have only shared with you concepts and strategies that I know to be proven to work, and you can rest assured knowing that these have been tested and proven on far more social media audiences than just mine. I share this information with you because I wish someone had broken it down like this for me when I was first starting out.

I hope you found the time you spent reading this chapter was well spent, as I understand your time is incredibly valuable.

Remember, all of social media is a game. A game of who has the most clearly defined message, who is the best at getting attention to that message, and who is the best at keeping that attention on their message through storytelling, cross promoting, and providing value to their audience.

The best message doesn't win. The message that is most clearly defined and simply stated does.

The best-looking content doesn't win. The content that gets the most attention does.

And the story that has the most value doesn't win, the one that keeps people engaged and coming back for more does.

As you sit down to plan out how you are going to apply these strategies to your own social media, I want to encourage you to study what others are doing, both inside and outside of your niche. Don't just look at the content they post, look at the strategy and storyline they are creating. Look at the big picture, the journey they are taking their audience on, and how it all fits together.

Thanks for choosing to spend your valuable time with me.

I am sure I will be seeing you soon on social media (@joshforti everywhere).

God bless,
Josh Forti

P.S. You're just one message away...

ABOUT JOSH FORTI

By the age of 24, Josh has made a statement in the world of social media and online marketing. Having co-owned an agency that grew and managed multiple million followers on Instagram, founded one of the fastest growing social media-related Facebook groups (Social Media For Entrepreneurs) with over 30,000+ members, and working with public figures and publications such as Grant Cardone, The Huffington Post, At GC-TV, Josh has proven his social media dominance and credibility time and time again.

Josh is also the co-founder of the social media software company Social Info, which provides accurate data analytics and market research tools allowing users to have the most up-to-date social media data for their accounts. Josh continues to provide education and tools to business owners and entrepreneurs that enable them to dominate their industry on social media and become recognized influencers.

Josh's "why" or purpose in life is to inspire others to break free and find their purpose, know truth, and define their own destiny, so they fall in love with life and make the world a better place.

contact@thinkdifferenttheory.com
thinkdifferenttheory.com

NOTES

NOTES

EMBRACING INFLUENCE AND INCOME ONLINE

by Darik Alexander

When embracing income and influence online, the biggest thing that must be understood is your positioning. It is such a busy world online, so you have to do whatever you can to not only break out of obscurity but do so while simultaneously coming out with the best content possible that will truly add value to your customer.

I have found that the best way to do that is understanding the three ways of scaling content and income online.

The first is to consistently come out with content in hopes that people will buy your product or service. This can be done through Facebook Lives, podcasts, YouTube, etc. The strategy is to do this long enough until hopefully people start buying what you have to offer. While many people use this strategy because it is the most predictable, long-term it can be exhausting if you don't have any predictable income coming into your business.

The second is to immediately do something that brings you income. This can be a coaching call, a live event, or launching a product. On one side you are making income by taking a specific action. However, the challenge is that as soon as the interaction is done, there is no more money. Once the event is over, you don't keep getting paid. Once the client-coach relationship is done, they stop paying you. So, it can be lucrative at times but also very stressful at others.

The last way, which I believe is the best, is to design a self-generating cash machine that can give you predictable income whether its large or small. You can then add the first and second strategies so that you can scale without the stress of wondering if your business is going to fail.

The best way to implement this strategy that I have seen in my career is to design a sequenced webinar funnel. Essentially, you design some type of product that can be sold without you needing to follow through with a high amount of responsibility. I recommend an online course that is targeted to your niche you choose to serve. Once the product is created, (I use Kajabi to host mine), you then need to design the offer that will make sure people are going to be inspired to purchase your product in the first place.

This process begins with designing your webinar. I use Russel Brunson's "The Perfect Webinar Script." take the content that is of value in your course and structure an offer using that script that will evoke your viewer to want to take some form of action. Please remember that when designing the webinar do not try to impress your viewer with tons of content but rather think of what are the one to three challenges you can solve in the webinar that will position you as an expert in your space.

Once you have designed your webinar, it is time to craft your sales funnel. This can be done in ClickFunnels, and I recommend creating some form of lead magnet that will attract your client. When thinking of a lead magnet, you want something that almost makes you feel skeptical that you should offer it for free. This helps identify that it is something that gives immense value. Once you have designed your lead magnet and the entire sales funnel, then it is time to run two different ad sets.

One will be an ad that goes directly to your lead magnet. Once they opt into your lead magnet, they will then be redirected to a page that invites them to register for your webinar. The second ad will go directly to the webinar registration. Once you have ads in place that are targeted to your specific market, you will begin to see purchases. Your goal is to consistently track these metrics and consistently scale. Ultimately, the lower your CPA (cost per acquisition), the more money you can put into buying customers and the larger your list will grow as well.

With this steady flow of cash flow coming in, it now lets you focus on the other two strategies we talked about previously. Coming out with consistent content over time to build your intrinsic value as well as taking immediate action through coaching, events or product launches. The idea is that when you combine these three methods together by first getting consistent cashflow with your webinar, you can position yourself in the marketplace to have longevity, which allows you to have influence, and most importantly, a long-lasting impact on those you are truly trying to serve.

ABOUT DARIK ALEXANDER

Darik is a highly profitable entrepreneur and trainer. As CEO of Ignite programs, he has worked with some of the top entrepreneurs in the world (including people like Gary Vaynerchuk, Darren Hardy, and Les Brown) and became a multiple six-figure earner at the age of 20, generating millions of dollars in revenue using offline and online marketing strategies.

His training programs have helped students attract thousands of qualified leads and sales through live events, online training, and coaching.

But it wasn't always this way for him. He was a broke college student, 50k in debt, and putting in long hours each day only to make $9 an hour at a concession stand. When he finally found a job working at a call center, he quickly learned he was meant for entrepreneurship when he received an 80-cent raise after being the top producer in the entire call center for 6 months straight. This lesson taught Darik that he needed to find a way out of the rat race now, or he would be stuck in it forever.

This is where he started his business and changed his life forever. Today, Darik has earned hundreds of thousands of dollars with a thriving business, amazing clients, and a dedicated team—and he's committed to helping entrepreneurs build their business using his simple, proven, heart-centered strategies.

darikalexander56@gmail.com
darikalexander.com

NOTES

NOTES

POVERTY TO 53 EMPLOYEES BY 20

by JR Rivas

I began my journey in entrepreneurship at 14. I grew up in a poor neighborhood with crime and the whole 9 yards. My high school had a 40% drop-out rate.

By 15, I was buying candy wholesale and selling it in school for $1. By 18, I started my first brick and mortar business. A tax business.

By 21, I had 3 locations and 53 employees. I then made my exit over the course of a few years.

I decided to start my digital marketing journey.

Now, at 24, I still feel like I'm just beginning to figure things out. Let me preface this chapter by saying this is the greatest time in human history to be an entrepreneur.

Naturally, with advancements in culture and technology come new challenges and problems. Now, I'm not going to talk about strategy in this chapter. On the surface, we all know the skills we need to learn to be successful by your own definition: get better at sales, get better at systems, get better at leading people, marketing, and so on. I want to give you something that will apply no matter what business you're in.

The reason we don't do the things that we know will push us forward is not because we're ignorant of them, we simply have mindset barriers.

If I told you to name three things you could do in the next 30 days that would radically change your life, it wouldn't be too hard to think of something, right?

Then why don't people just do that?

Mindset.

Mindset doesn't work through logic. If it did, you could just tell yourself to do the things that would make your life better, and you'd do them. Mindset works through conditioning. It's a process. So, I'm going to share the top three mindset shifts that I believe will help you achieve anything you want from this life.

1. DISCIPLINE

Everything you want is on the other side of discipline. Intuitively, you know what to do to get a six-pack. Everyone does since the era of google began. But why isn't everyone walking around shredded? Because we lack discipline. Like Navy Seal Jocko Willink says, "Discipline equals freedom." With discipline, you can master anything, acquire anything, and literally build the person you want to be.

For me, discipline finds its light with routine. We are creatures of habit, so make good ones and work to kill bad ones.

It's a journey in and of itself.

We all have that highest version of ourselves in our minds.

You know who that is for you, that "super hero" version of yourself. That person that wakes up early and works out, stays focused, gets shit done, shows up at work and at home, and is constantly improving. The person that makes people wonder, "How does he do it?"

The good news is that person already lives inside of you, but like a sculpture, you have to chip away the garbage to reveal it. You literally have to almost kill the person you are to reveal him or her. That person lives on the other side of discipline.

2. MENTAL TOUGHNESS

This one is tough for people. As humans, we have this innate desire for life to be easy: six-minute abs, make money with the click of a button, get dates without leaving your house or even talking to anyone ever. Why are those ideals so popular and attractive? Because they work.

See, here's the thing. Without mental toughness, you will fold at the first sign of adversity, the first time you run into a roadblock and, God forbid, something really tragic happens. If you haven't been training your mind to get tougher, how will you handle the loss of a loved one, a dip in the economy, or any other hard situation.

My philosophy for developing this is to do things that scare you or make you uncomfortable.

For a while, I was afraid of getting punched in the face. Kind of silly, I know. I'm not particularly confrontational, so the odds of that happening were low, but I knew that facing a fear gives you xp points (for my gamers out there) toward mental toughness.

How did I confront this?

I started doing jiu jitsu and boxing. Getting choked, punched, and constantly tapped out made me realize it's not as bad as I thought.

I think David Goggins put it best in his interview with the Unbeatable Mind podcast. I'm paraphrasing but it went something like this:

"Be that one motherfucker. Be that one guy that, when all hell's breaking loose and even the toughest motherfuckers are looking around to be led, be that one motherfucker that just says fuck it and brings the other hundred of the world's toughest motherfuckers home."

I live my life in pursuit that, of being that one motherfucker.

A good practice of strengthening mental toughness is to give up complaining. Not just audibly, but in your own mind. Tell yourself *I will not complain* constantly. Ritualize it. Complaining is the cousin of excuses. It opens the door for excuses and invites them into your mind.

Let me give you an example. A few weeks ago, I was catching a flight in Tampa and decided to stay at a buddy's house. On the way there, he tells me, "Hey, our AC literally just went out." I got there, and my bed was a leather couch. Leather has a reputation for not being the most breathable of materials and especially not when it's 95 degrees in Florida.

This could have been an easy opportunity for me to complain, have a bad attitude, and a bad night's sleep—if I would have allowed it. This surely would have carried over into the next day and transition itself into a "bad day." Instead, I decided to say *fuck it* and refuse to let complaining creep into my mind.

I spent my life in pursuit of comfort, now I fear being too comfortable.

3. EMPATHY AND SELF-AWARENESS

I group these two together because empathy is feeling what other people feel, while self-awareness is being conscious of what you feel and who you are. The best business people I've met are the most empathetic. They understand the motives of others and understand that the key to getting what they want is to truly want to help others get what they want. That's where empathy comes in.

I believe this comes from dealing with enough people and taking a step back to truly understand what gets them up in the morning. It's almost like the most successful people have naturally mastered this skill.

I am not someone who's mastered this, nor am I a natural. My way of understanding others is through always asking *why*. This is one of the most powerful questions in the English language. Ask *why* enough times to see who someone really is, what they really care about, and what gets them excited.

Self-awareness works kind of the same way, but instead, you have to ask yourself *why* constantly. This can be uncomfortable because you'll face some not-so-pretty parts of yourself. Some examples of asking yourself why in a productive way are as follows.

Why did I say I was going to do something, but then I didn't do it?

Why didn't my actions in this particular instance not match up with my goals or the person I want to be?

Why did that certain action trigger that feeling?

Why are these my goals?

Why did I make that decision?

Why, why, why?

The more you ask yourself *why*, the closer you'll get to who you truly want to be and deciding who that is.

The key is to be honest.

For example, if you ask yourself, *Why do I want to be a millionaire?* and your answer is *So others will see my value*, then your next question is *Why do I feel that way?* And so on.

Once you know what truly motivates you and can spend time with your insecurities, it's a much clearer path to becoming the superhero version of yourself.

I am in no way saying that I've mastered these pursuits. Like you, I am on this same journey.

Whether you decide to work on these things for yourself or not, at least now you are aware.

ABOUT JR RIVAS

At age 14, I went 6 months without running water, and it was the best thing that ever happened to me because it lit a fire—I wanted to make a lot of money. I looked around at the people giving me advice in life (mainly teachers), and I knew that if I listened to them, I would only get what they had. I wanted to be wealthy and set myself and my family up for generations to come. So, I began to investigate and learn. What I found was that success was a recipe, not a random lucky draw. By the time I was 18, I had opened up my first brick and mortar business, a tax office. I quickly grew that to 3 locations and 53 employees by the time I was 21. I knew this wasn't what I wanted to do forever, so I sold the business and dove head first into digital marketing. I quickly scaled to 6 figures within 45 days of landing my first Facebook Ads client. From there, I expanded my consulting practice to what it is today with clients in over 35 countries. Now, I am expanding into helping entrepreneurs a different way—through bettering their bodies in the weight room to prepare for the war every day known as business.

NOTES

MILLION-DOLLAR BRANDING ON A SHOE-STRING BUDGET

by Sonya Lee

B randing is a powerful thing. Used correctly, it creates trust, draws an emotional response, and attracts customers effortlessly. What most people fail to understand is that branding is more than just a logo, picking out a few colors, or fancy fonts.

Billion-dollar companies are constantly investing, seeking to unlock the magic combination that endlessly attracts high-paying, loyal customers. They have massive marketing departments with budgets running into the millions dedicated to squeezing out every last penny they can. And having spent more than 20 years in the industry with the likes of Warner Brothers and Disney (who later became *my* clients, btw...), I can assure you that branding yields magical results when applied strategically.

Except you and I don't have billion-dollar companies with million-dollar marketing departments. Even fewer of us can afford to randomly invest time or money like that in the hopes we'll ever find our own secret combination that attracts the masses.

What, then, are we to do? Obviously, there's something to this method, but are we like David facing Goliath? Are we just chum in the water waiting to be devoured by the sharks? Is it just luck of the draw?

Well, first off, relax! It's actually not so difficult once you understand the formula, and you're about to learn that. And further, David had a strategy, Goliath was mostly blind, sharks rarely attack humans, and it's an awesome cliché that "the harder I work, the luckier I get."

You see, Warner Brothers was my first real job after design school when I was just 19. That time in my life gave me hands-on experience and corporate insights to some of the world's greatest brands including Harry Potter, Looney Tunes, TrueCar, Disney, Adobe, Cisco, and more. Most importantly, it paved the way for my journey into entrepreneurship and allowed me to work with some of the most prominent and respected tech visionaries and investors.

Four jobs and six businesses later, I now get paid to help corporations and entrepreneurs make more money through strategic branding, marketing, and user-experience. And this is what I've picked up along the way about brands.

A brand is tailored experience designed specifically for your customers. It is not about you at all. Your brand dictates how your customers will see, think, feel, remember, and do business with you. This is highly important because we all buy based on emotion and then use logic to back our decision. That's *a lot* more than just logos, colors, and fonts.

Billion-dollar businesses know this and often win over customers *before* the sales process has even begun. They know that strategically tapping into the emotions of their most loyal and committed customers creates an investment that keeps on going even long after the sale has been made.

That's the nutshell version of branding. It's not too complicated, and the results speak for themselves.

So to answer the question brewing in your mind, here are the 10 key steps to unlocking your own million-dollar brand. I promise, it's not as intimidating as it might seem!

1. **Identify a Niche Segment**

   In order to set yourself apart, carve out a unique position for yourself in your industry. Also, identify a very specific type of customer you want to work with. Specificity is of absolute importance here, so let's get super clear about *what you do* and *who your high-paying customers are.*

2. **Same, but Different**

   Your brand needs to offer *a unique customer opportunity to experience a lifestyle, benefit, or inherent value.* It's not that your product or service alone isn't good enough, it's about signaling to your customer that you have a superior process, formula, method, or insights. Your unique "thing" promises that only you can help them.

3. **Heighten the Senses with Emotion**
   The easiest and fastest way to appeal to your customer is through authentic storytelling. Why? Because it humanizes your business and helps your customer resonate and connect with you. I know that storytelling seems counter-intuitive, but the opposite is true. What's the backstory to your business, and how did you get where you are today?

4. **Study Exclusivity**
   Branding is never created in a vacuum or in a split second. It takes time, effort, and energy. A shortcut to great branding is to study other successful competitors in your industry and businesses who share the same audience. What we're looking for are insights on their branding and marketing tactics.

   For example, as a digital marketer, you may want to study Seth Godin, Gary Vee, Neil Patel and perhaps *Entrepreneur* and *Fortune* magazines. Carefully study their words, colors, fonts, designs, styles, messaging, and positioning, as well as its essence, aura, and how it makes you feel.

5. **Design Exclusivity**
   Next, go to Pinterest and create a visual mood board of all the things you've learned about your competitors that work for your business. Gathering these cues will help you visualize and create your own unique brand. Once you're finished, work with a graphic designer to create an appealing, high-end brand that borrows from the successes of others. Don't forget to include your story!

6. **Inspire Belonging**
   Big businesses and high-end brands have in common a sense of ownership or community with their customers. The more

engagement your business can create organically, the better. Your customers want to feel like they're the only person in the world that matters. Let's help them to get closer with you.

7. **Superior Brand Promise**
   Once your customer buys in, you must deliver on all promises in every single sense. Your business has a reputation to manage, and it had better be consistent every single time. Remember, it's much easier to maintain a great relationship than it is to repair a broken one.

8. **Create the High-End Journey**
   Your customers live on a dynamic, moving timeline, not a fixed one. With your newfound insights, map out a positive and productive experience that fully anticipates the needs of your customer from start to finish. A good example of a journey is an incredible hotel experience that begins from the moment you arrive at the hotel and all the way through receiving a customer satisfaction survey days after your departure.

9. **Remember Your Manners**
   It's *crucial* that you treat your customers with constant respect. You literally wouldn't have a business without them, so show them your appreciation. It will go a long way and reinforce your million-dollar brand for years to come. The return on investment with good manners (free) is word-of-mouth marketing.

10. **Treat Your Brand Like A Person**
    Finally, treat your million-dollar brand like a living, breathing, flexible identity. The more you apply these strategic approaches, the more your brand will evolve with clear insights. Over time, you'll learn how to easily tap into the emotions of your customers by studying what works and what doesn't.

As you can see, branding is more psychological than it is operational. Obviously there is strategy involved but following this outline will help you far more effectively invest your time, money, and energy to build your own million dollar brand. Combine a bit of elbow grease and empathy for your audience with consistent effort, and you can create a memorable experience for your customers from day one. As you dial in the right formula to captivate and attract your customers, your brand will continue working for you even when you're asleep. And that, my friend, is when it just gets fun.

ABOUT SONYA LEE

Sonya Lee is a keynote speaker, UX expert, and business coach in Orange County, California.

By age 26, she became an award-winning web designer and has the honor of being called "disruptive" when helping Bob Iger, the CEO of Disney, launch Disney.com. She has worked on brands for Warner Bros, AT&T, TrueCar, Adobe, and Cisco and launched several tech companies.

With more than 20 years of experience in branding, marketing, technology, and startups, she now helps Fortune 100 companies and entrepreneurs increase revenue by developing campaigns and messages that persuade and attract customers.

At an early age, Sonya was sent to live in a monastery that left her emotionally scarred and struggling to know her true self. Being cut off from mainstream society initially stunted her growth, but rather than shrink back, she used the experience to push the boundaries of personal evolution and improve the human experience. Sonya is also the founder of UX Your Life™, a personal development framework designed to maximize the human potential.

info@sonyalee.io
www.sonyalee.io

NOTES

NOTES

HOW TO SCALE YOUR INFLUENCE AND INCOME RAPIDLY WITH A FACEBOOK GROUP

by Arne Giske

Have you ever wondered what the difference is between the online entrepreneurs that make it big and the ones that get stuck earning just a little bit but are never really scaling up and thriving?

I'm Arne Giske, and that's exactly where I was at a few years ago—confused, stuck, and not happy with my level of influence and income. I knew there had to be an easier way to make this whole online business thing work, so I started searching to see what the secret sauce was that a lot of successful entrepreneurs had in common.

It wasn't the fancy funnels, the professional headshots and logos, the media appearances, or the content they blasted out online. It was something much simpler: they had an audience of raving fans and cultivated that audience using a Facebook group.

I've had ugly funnels, no website, a pretty plain logo, and I'm terrible at tech setups, but I relied on building my Facebook group to be the best one on the planet for the people I'm serving.

After four failed groups and then growing the fifth one to over 72,000 members in just two years, it's helped add multiple six figures in sales and over 1,500 customers to my business. The crazy thing is, I didn't even have to pay for ads to grow the group—Facebook does that for you organically!

Want to uncover how to get Facebook to promote your group constantly so you can grow your audience into the thousands and build your tribe of raving fans who know, like, trust, and PAY you constantly?

You're in the right place. In this chapter, I'll be uncovering my top growth hacks to get a ton of people in the door to your group ASAP, even if you're just getting started. Ready to roll?

First up, your personal Facebook profile needs a makeover. We call this the "Profile Funnel."

- Design a cover photo that speaks to your target market and invites them to your group

- Edit your bio to include an elevator pitch showing exactly who you help and how

- Update your featured photo to pitch the group as well

- Edit your About section and add a link to your FB group where it says "website"

- Try out what I call a Bait Post where you tease some content and say something like "Do you want to learn how I got X result in X days? Leave a comment, and I'll invite you to my FB group where I show you how!"

This profile funnel is the easiest way to grow because if you're constantly active online, people will click on your name, land on your profile, and get linked to your group. Pretty cool, huh?

Next up, the #1 thing that will make or break your organic group growth is the name of the group. When you browse FB, you see the "suggested groups" category pop up occasionally, and you want your group name to stand out. People scroll quickly, and if they don't know why your group is relevant in the first two seconds of seeing it, they won't click to join.

Here's an exercise to optimize that for FB search and the suggested groups feature:

The first three words need to be keyword / identity heavy. An example would be my group, "Millennial Entrepreneur Community" versus "Arne's Awesome Hangout Club For Millennial Entrepreneurs."

Brainstorm five possible keywords (words that reflect that topics of the group), five possible identity words (phrases your target market immediately identifies with), and play around with putting them together.

Last but not least, you're going to set up your "growth spiderweb" to trap everyone who comes across you online! This way you maximize every opportunity to grow your group.

Here is a list of places to add your FB group link and invite people:

- A Community button/banner on your website

- Link in your email footer (both personal emails and mass emails)

- Link on any thank you pages after someone opts in

- Link on your chatbot if you have one

- Link on any other social channel bios (Twitter, Instagram, Quora, etc.)

But most importantly, you want to include a short pitch for *why* they should join the group. This will help filter in the right people and increase your growth rates.

Overall, growing a Facebook group is the simplest part, but getting engagement, building a brand, and monetizing the group is a bit more of a challenge.

Get started with the growth for now and check out fbgroupsforbusiness.com to uncover some more strategies for monetizing and more!

"Grow Your Group, Grow Your Business!"

- Arne Giske

ABOUT ARNE GISKE

 Arne Giske is a serial entrepreneur, speaker, and digital agency owner who leads The Millennial Entrepreneur Community with over 73,000 young members around the globe. He travels all over the world while he builds his business and went to eleven countries and a dozen states in 2017!

He helps other entrepreneurs build strong businesses using effective digital marketing strategies such as growing communities online with Facebook groups to build their audience, brand, and generate tons of new leads consistently.

After failing to build groups four times, he dedicated himself to learning what it would take to build an amazing community that also fueled his business growth and now teaches others to do the same.

support@arnegiske.org
fbgroupsforbusiness.com

NOTES

NOTES

ATTRACTING YOUR IDEAL CLIENT FOR FREE

by Akbar Sheikh

All right, so you want to make it online. Start off by asking what your skills are. You might know what you're good at already. If not, fine tune it. Spend some time in review materials or read some books. Just sharpen your tools a little bit before trying to get at it online.

Your next step to starting your online business is identifying who can benefit immensely from these skills. Realize that this whole, this whole game is nothing but "problem" and "solution". I have the solution in my skillset. Now I just need to go find the people who have that problem I can provide the solution for.

My skillset is mindset, copy, and funnels. Lucky for me, there are lots of people out there who need help.

"Oh, I don't know how to make a good funnel."
"Oh, I don't know how to write good copy."
"Oh, I don't know what kind of mindset I should be happy."

For me, those people are typically marketers and entrepreneurs.

We are very fortunate that no matter what industry you're in, people have problems. Now there's something called Facebook groups that are very profitable. Here's what's gonna happen. People ask questions. You go answer them. And give them real, seriously valuable responses. Go and search Facebook and find the best groups for that particular niche.

Questions to ask yourself:

- How many people are in the group? It should be over a thousand people.

- Look what the engagement is. Are people engaging in these posts? Are people giving each other value? Or is it just kind of like anything goes and there's a bunch of spam?

- Are the kinds of expert positioning posts you want to do allowed?

So, you go into these groups, and you'll see that 99% of the people are asking the same questions. Let's say you're in the health niche.

"Hey, how do I get a six pack?"

Let's just say you're awesome at getting people in the best shape of their lives in the health industry. Then there's a question or a group: "Who can get me the best shape of my life?"

Now, this is a very powerful question for several reasons. Number one, obviously the person is asking the question. Number one: It's a red hot lead. They are looking for that solution, that result.

Number two: There's a ton of other people following the question who also want to get in the best shape of their life too, so they're keeping an eye on the answers.

Now, this is where you're lucky. Most people in there say, "Me, me, me, me, me!"

Useless.

So you've got to understand that most people are lazy. You think I'm going to go in there and investigate every single person? No, of course not. I'm going to pick the person who gave the best response.

"Hey man, I can help you get in the best shape a life. Actually, I've helped several people get in the best shape of their life, or I've been helping people get in the best shape of their life since 1991."

There's a little authority in there too. But if you don't have a lot of proof, don't say how they even did it or that you've done it for a long time, but if you've been doing it for that long, you should have proof anyway, but you see, you start giving value.

"Oh, by the way, one thing, we drink a lot of good water because that will get you hydrated, which will deplete your fat cells, and then we give you a special mushroom that kills the veins that nourish your fat. And by the way, we don't exercise too much. I hope you don't mind. We just do some light stretching." (Obviously, I'm not a health coach!)

I want to lose the weight. I don't want to exercise. And you can make that happen? Winner!

Not only are you going to get that dude as a client, but you can get several others. You'll find most groups really aren't very good and you've got to really spend time to identify the best ones.

Since you're giving me so much good advice, reciprocity kicks in and people just get magnetized towards you, the leader, the person who is giving valuable content. They're going to send you a friend request. Accept it and then start a conversation.

Now that you've been answering all those questions now, within a few days, people will start contacting you.

So you accept their friend request and say, "Hey, how can I help you get into the best shape of your life?"

Just get right to it. Don't do any small talk. Get right to the chase. Nobody will mind because everybody wants results. Nobody cares where you're from, where your aunt lives, nobody cares where you went to high school.

What's really happening now is that more traffic is coming to your Facebook profile page. That's what organic marketing is. Now you need to optimize your Facebook banner. You might say something like "Helping people get six packs since 1991" or whatever the case is. Make sure it's a picture with authority, and it explains exactly what you do. If you're teaching people about six packs… you should probably have a six pack and show that.

Next up, your bio. A lot of people put these useless things like "world traveler" or "serial entrepreneur" or "I like cats." Nobody cares. Inject more authority and credibility here.

"Certified Health Coach"
"Olympic qualifier"
"healthcoachasdf.com"

Lastly, make sure your website or funnel is linked at the bottom of your profile.

So up until now, you've just been answering questions, which is good, but there's another way where you can draw even more attention to yourself, especially now that you've had these conversations. You can see the commonalities and comment publicly on them. The kind of post you're about to do is called a value post. Now you're going to have to identify which groups allow you to give each other value. Every day you should be doing at least two value posts. Don't sell anything. Just post nothing but give pure value.

"Here's a little golden nugget. Water is good for you, but it's very hard to drink a gallon of water a day. Here's an awesome little trick to get it done."

People get a little bit of benefit from you. Now, what's going to end up happening is you're actually building a team of salespeople right now because you're just giving all this value.

Then the cycle begins again. People start asking questions. "Hey, who's the best guy to get me in shape?" People you've never even met are going to start tagging you and say, "This guy knows what he's talking about!" That *third party* social proof is... you can't even buy that kind of credibility, and you'll get a ton of business.

This is the plan to get like a ton of organic business. It's through these conversations that you can make those first sales.

Now it's up to you. You can either coach people (which doesn't really cost anything for setup), or you can sell people a digital course. This is made so much easier with a ClickFunnels account. If you have a computer or even an iPhone, you can record your screen and go over slides. Some of the best courses I've taken in my life are just slideshows. Making an online course is really no big deal at all.

"How can I help your business grow?"

Let's say you're working in funnels:

"Hey, show me your funnel."

(They send you a link.)

"Oh my God, the checkout page is missing this. This testimony is useless. Oh my God, the copy is terrible."

Truth is, they're going to know all this, and I'm going to agitate their pain.

"You're spending all this money on Facebook. This is why you're not converting. You see that, right?"

"Yes, of course, of course I see that."

Then, I'm going to paint them a picture of what their success can be. As them, "What do you want to be earning?"

Predictably, they're going to say a million dollars.

"Why?"

D'oh. They didn't talk about that.

"Okay, well what would life be like if you were to get there?"

We're still painting the picture here. We're getting them into imagine life that way.

Next up, you just tell them how you can help them with that EXACT problem. Close them. Put them on a coaching deal. Work with them one on one to help them scale their business. Then they're going to ask about pricing...

Now remember, right now I have no fame. I've got no list. I've got nothing. So I have to start a little small, and that's okay. So here's the offer you're going to give them:

"Hey, man I want to work with you, and I want to give you this amazing deal. I'm actually in the process of building case studies. I'm going to give you something called case study-based pricing. The everyday price for all this is $70,000. Okay? But I'm in the process of collecting case studies, so if you're ready to make a deal right now and promise to give me a complete case study when you're getting the kind of results you're looking for, then I'm literally going to knock off half of the investment."

Whether you close them or not, stop there for the day. That's a lot. And you'll be doing a lot of these calls. You might fail for a while until you make your first sale. Do NOT give up.

If you're not closing deals, you need to show more social proof. You need to show more testimonies. How am I going to get testimonies?

Well, I've got all these friends now on my Facebook profile, and all these people know I'm in the funnel game. They know I'm in the online entrepreneur space. So now I'm going to say, "Hey guys, guess what? This is insane. My services are very expensive, but I'm actually building a brand. I want to get some brand new case studies. For the next three people who comment, 'Yes, give it to me,' I'm actually going to critique their funnel for free."

Also include their qualifications. "You have to have a front-end offering; you have to be having a budget since free to send ads on. It needs to be having something viable that you've sold before but you're just stuck on."

What happens next? "Yes, yes, yes." People comment.

Now, there's one more qualification for these people. They need to act fast on this stuff, so make sure that's in the post. The beautiful part about any of this stuff is that things work relatively quickly. You'll get two or three people, and you can get to work right away.

So you get on a call, and whatever field you're in, I'm just telling you what to do. Then they're going to get results almost immediately they're going to be floored immediately. They're going to be so grateful because they didn't pay anything.

Remember reciprocity. Now you ask if they can record a quick testimony for you, and they'll absolutely do it!

"I just went over everything with Akbar, and oh my God, I am floored. I feel like I have a seven-figure blueprint. We changed my entire business. I now have clarity. I now have direction."

Before… I was here… during… service was amazing… after… I had clarity.

Now, you've got all these testimonies for free, and it just costs a little bit of time. Take those testimonials, throw them up on a quick landing page, and put up quick scheduling page.

The scheduling page is going to have a little form that's going to ask all the right questions to *prequalify* your ideal customer because you only want to work with your ideal customer and no one else.

These strategies are universal. You can do this strategy on Facebook groups. You can do this strategy on LinkedIn. You can do this strategy on Instagram. Do it where your target market is. You need to just rinse and repeat in order to keep growing your organic reach.

ABOUT AKBAR SHEIKH

Akbar Sheikh is a #1 international best-selling author, speaker, master of the 7 Ethical Principles of Persuasion, has helped 7 funnels hit 7 figures, father, and philanthropist with a concentration on orphans and giving the gift of vision to blind children.

Prior, he was homeless, overweight, in a terrible relationship, and suffered from a crippling anxiety disorder.

He does what he does because he believes that entrepreneurs are inherently good people that want to make more revenue thus they can give to their families, communities, and favorite charities, hence making the world a better place.

Akbar is on a mission to use persuasion for good, helping people break through, the ethical way.

akbar@akbarsheikh.com
akbarsheikh.com

NOTES

MAKE MONEY WITH BOOKS AND BOOKLETS
(EVEN IF YOU'VE NEVER WRITTEN BEFORE)

by Chris O'Byrne

They say that content is king. They say you should publish a lot of content to establish your brand and grow your business. They're right!

And a book, especially a print book, is the most effective content out there. Just having your book listed on Amazon is a huge form of social proof that shows you really do know what you're talking about. They're no longer saying that print books will become obsolete. In fact, print books are more important (and valuable) than ever before. With a print book, your potential customer has your billboard advertising your brand and your business that sits on their desk or bookshelf, constantly reminding them of you.

Ebooks are also relevant and valuable. Most people read ebooks on their phones, now. Imagine someone readying your book while they're waiting in line or traveling or whenever they have a few minutes. I do that all of the time, and so do most people that I know.

There are three secrets to writing a book that grabs people's attention and makes them glad they bought your book.

The first secret is to use copywriting techniques. Good copywriting is essential to grab the attention of your potential customers. And long form content, long sales letters, are the most effective form of copywriting. When you write a book, you create a way for your potential customer to read great copywriting without even realizing that's what they're reading. They receive big value, and you transform hundreds of people from being merely interested into people that believe in you.

The second secret is to teach. Don't just write a bunch of facts and think that you're teaching people. You're not actually teaching unless someone is learning. You want to understand how the learning process works and what helps people understand and retain what you're teaching. We don't just learn because we're reading facts, we learn because a connection is made in our brains to other facts and because we're engaged. Take the time to learn how people learn.

The third secret is to tell stories. Stories help us engage, which opens us up to accepting what we learn. Longer stories that weave facts and experience are especially helpful, but so even short anecdote can engage your audience. I used to teach middle and high school and whenever I told stories that illustrated certain points, my students would pay attention. They also would do far better on tests for those topics that came from the stories I told.

Next, when you publish your book, don't just put your book on Amazon and expect it to sell. And don't just mention it on Facebook and hope it will sell. You need to make sure that your target audience knows about your book. They need to see how reading your book will improve their lives or take away their pain. This is where you use your copywriting skills again.

I suggest both selling your book on Amazon and selling your book on your own site using the free + shipping model! With the f+s model, you give away your book for free and the customer only pays for shipping. This not only gets your book into your potential customer's hands, but it gives you an opportunity to upsell during the process. Most people have to pay to get leads for their business. With the f+s model where you have a chance to upsell other products or services, you actually make money, often a lot of money, while you're gaining new leads.

And, for the people who only buy the book and none of your upsells, you still get them on your mailing list. Which means you have many more chances to bring value to them and turn them into a happy customer.

Last, you need to send traffic to both your book on Amazon and your free + shipping funnel on your website. Remember, these are two different audiences. For people who find your book on Amazon because they are searching for a book like yours, use Amazon Ads. Amazon has their own advertising platform that you can use to greatly increase how many people find and buy your book on Amazon.

For your free + shipping book, use Facebook Ads, Google Ads, Instagram, and so on to send traffic to that funnel. Two different audiences means two different approaches to advertising.

If you're ready to massively grow your brand or your business by writing and publishing your own expert book (or even a booklet), then I encourage you to email me at chris@jetlaunch.net to learn more. Take action today, and you'll have big results tomorrow.

ABOUT CHRIS O'BYRNE

Chris O'Byrne's mission is to help *you* change lives by writing and publishing a life-changing book—or booklet. And it's much easier than you think!

To learn more about booklets, you can just head on over to **jetlaunchbooklets.com**

If you want to learn how to make money from your book or booklet, go to **facebook.com/groups/buildauthority**

chris@jetlaunch.net
jetlaunch.net

NOTES

NOTES

THE 10-FIGURE MINDSET

by David Wolff

So, you have an idea that's destined for greatness. All you have to do is execute, but where should you begin? Where will you use all of that energy you'll put into that great idea? Before you race in the wrong direction toward failure along with almost everyone else, you need to take a minute and listen to another approach to business. It's a way that actually works. You need to know how to think and succeed big, really big. You need to have a 10-figure mindset to be as successful as you possibly can.

Let's start off with the mistake that dooms most people before they get started—thinking small. When asked how much money people want to make many reply "a million dollars" but how do you know your full potential is a million dollars? It could be a 100 million, a billion, or more. Others will answer "as much as I can" but being vague is just as big of a problem. You need to decide just how big you want to be from the beginning so the actions you take match the size of your vision. Set a goal that is unreachable right now so you are forced to stretch way outside your comfort zone. An example of stretching yourself is Arthur Guinness when he signed a 9,000-year lease when he started his brewery. Highly successful people reach far beyond their grasp knowing it is going to take personal growth, hard work, and calculated risk on their part to achieve those goals, so aim as high as you dare, then farther still. Get uncomfortable.

To accomplish your newly set goals, you need to avoid traits others consider normal business behavior. Grinding all hours of the day and late into the night won't get you to really big goals, but it will destroy your health, personal relationships, and overall happiness. You need to get up early take care of yourself and your family, then once at work, your most important tasks must be done by 11:00 a.m. Your mind simply doesn't function well after the first 5 to 6 hours of the day. Multitasking is something everyone agrees is what you do to succeed but all it really does is give you a long list of failures. Focus on one task at a time, complete it, then move on. Last is the idea that there are many important tasks to get done. It's just not true and thinking this way will have you stuck in the 90% of work that doesn't make you money. Only 10% of the work you do determines 80% to 90% of the success you have. Stay in that highly productive 10%.

So how do you know what's in your 10%? It's very simple. Just take a look back at the high goal you set for your business. Take that end goal and work backward in time to set other shorter-term goals you need to accomplish. If you want a 10-figure business, it's going to take a few years to get there. It's a distant goal, so think about where you need to be in 5 years to have a shot at it. Then create 3-year, 1-year, monthly, weekly, and finally, a daily goal. You need a picture of the path you're taking to reach your end goal. Now, look at your daily goal and ask yourself this: Of all the tasks you have to do, which one or two, when finished, complete your daily goal. You will find there's really only 1, maybe 2, to work on. Keep track of your progress toward your weekly and monthly goals as well. This is the only task to do during your important morning work. You're now in your 10%, and you can do anything if you stay there.

Staying in your 10% requires always knowing your most important task, setting a morning time block to work on it, and forming the habit of doing this every day. I learned about time blocking early in my career, and after the 10%, it is the second most important reason for my success. If you don't plan your time out in blocks and ignore the interruptions, you will fall out of your 10% every day. If you time block and protect that time, after 45 to 60 days you will form a habit, and it will become easy to remain productive. I know this was brief, but I wanted to tell you how a 10-figure mindset works and how different it is from how everyone else conducts business. It's the reason only a few achieve great success while everyone else falls well short. The 10-figure mindset works, and I'm living proof of it. You can be, too, so get going TODAY!

ABOUT DAVID WOLFF

David started out young in real estate achieving great success quickly. He received numerous awards including Rookie of the Year, Top Producer, #1 Team, #1 Group, and $100 Million Producer Club.

David opened his own real estate firm which quickly grew from one office and 34 agents to offices in 12 states with over 1,000 agents and 100 employees. He also started his own title and mortgage entity, escrow service, and business consulting firm.

David's businesses reached over $1 billion dollars in sales for 5 consecutive years averaging $345 million in annual revenue before being sold.

During that time, David helped 350+ agents reach seven figures in income as their full-time mentor. Helping others achieve success became David's passion which he's still involved in today.

David is a father of 4 and has been married for 20 years. He's traveled to 42 countries and says traveling to different parts of the world helped him greatly to understand and work with people from different backgrounds and points of view.

david@davidjwolff.com
davidjwolff.com

NOTES

THE THREE PROVEN CORE PRINCIPLES TO BUILDING, SCALING, AND KEEPING YOUR BUSINESS

by Kolton Krottinger

Hey, it's Kolton.... Kolton Krottinger! I am so honored to share some golden nuggets that have helped me go from blowing into a breathalyzer to getting a bunk at a homeless shelter to landing my dream woman on stage and building a real 7-figure business that impacts lives around the world!

I was the guy who got injured in the military and experienced some traumatic events and spent a year locked into a bedroom with extreme PTSD, waking up in ambulances from severe panic attacks.

When I say severe, I mean my hands and feet went numb every day. One of the most embarrassing stories of my PTSD attacks was that I could not dial 911 with my hands and had to crawl on my arms and legs to the neighbor's house, hitting my head on their front door, crying and screaming for them to dial 911.

I tell you this story because I was on 14 medications, was clinically insane, couldn't be around people, and couldn't drive a car. One doctor told my mom that I should be institutionalized because I couldn't function as a normal member of society.

Right before I had almost given up entirely on life, I decided I needed to get out of this situation if I wanted to live. I stopped getting distracted by everything and focused on one thing and one thing only that saved me—MINDSET.

Mindset was the key I used to open up the most incredible doors in life, and it started with me being able to function as a human being because I had a dream that I was destined to do something great with my life.

As you might know, some of the biggest moments that helped me get where I am today are the mentorships and coaching programs I received along the way. Before that, I spent seven years struggling trying to make it on my own.

I have partnered up with the one and only James Smiley to bring you the most disruptive coaching program on the planet. This was a major shift in my life. Rather than just trying to create solutions like I had done for seven years and 34 failed businesses, I focused on *one* major problem and how to solve it.

If I'm going to be honest, 90–95% of coaching programs and courses are not delivering. I've seen it, I've been there, and I've felt what it's like to have my back against the wall.

People need a return on their investment; they need real advice. People putting their last dollar out there asking for help need a leader who delivers! I've been let down. I've had my girlfriend leave me because I invested everything into the dream, and it never took off. I get it, I promise you.

I knew in my heart this was the problem I wanted to focus on, and when we created the solution, it practically sold itself with a six-figure pre-launch.

One thing I learned in the military is that we share the burden together. I have a "no man or woman left behind" policy. What kind of strong policy can you have in your business? Do you see the difference in mindset?

You see, for the past seven years, I wanted to deliver solutions, and that's what kept me broke. The moment I shifted my mindset into a "moral obligation" to help as many people as I possibly could with a "no man or woman left behind" policy, my business absolutely exploded.

It's funny how that works, isn't it? A simple shift in my mindset changed everything for me. This is where I lead into my three core principles to success. Obviously, before making money with my principles, you must have an offer, so I'm assuming you've got that. If you don't, I suggest reading Russell Brunson's book *Expert Secrets*; focus on your hook, story, and offer; and then adopt my principles as your own.

The first core principle is MINDSET. I've broken this down into financial goals to help you focus on the right principal at the right time. If you are making less than $10k a month, I would focus solely on mindset. It is so easy to get distracted by shiny object syndrome in the beginning stages of entrepreneurship—believe me.

I remember going to sleep every night with my laptop on my chest focusing on banners, websites, social media, etc. You know, all the stuff they tell you to do that does not matter at the end of the day when you are starting out.

You miss so many opportunities when your sights are on the wrong target. This reminds me of the gun shoots in the military. We each had our own rifle, and some men and women took a lot of pride in their rifle. They cleaned it until it looked brand new, they bought expensive gun slings, carrying cases, and all the bells and whistles you could imagine.

I must admit, my rifle did not look the prettiest, and all I did was spray some gun oil on it before a shoot to keep it lubricated and operating correctly.

There was one spot for sniper school and 20 of us on the line. I talked to nobody, I wasn't showboating my gear, I focused on one thing and one thing only—the target. I beat everyone there and took that spot in sniper school. My mindset was the only thing I focused on and that's what got me the outcome I needed.

Again, if you are making less than $10k a month, focus on mindset and don't get distracted by shiny objects. Make the $10k mark your target and go get it!

The next core principle is MARKETING. This is what you focus on when your mindset is on point and you have a business generating at least $10k to $100k a month.

Marketing becomes so much easier when your mindset is on point because you now have a converting hook, story, and offer generating at least $10k a month. I'm not talking about Facebook ads or Google AdWords; I'm talking about getting out there in front of as many eyeballs as possible.

When you get into the marketing phase, it's simply a numbers game at this point, and I love numbers. My focus is guerilla marketing, and I want to urge you to give it a try for yourself because it works extremely well when you get the concept down.

Guerilla marketing is defined as "innovative, unconventional, and low-cost marketing techniques aimed at obtaining maximum exposure for a product." Sounds pretty fancy, right? I like to tell people it's a fancy way of finding a way to market while being broke.

Now, I'm not saying that you or I are broke, but we're here to have healthy businesses with good profit margins so we can keep fueling the machine. Does that make sense?

I'm going to quickly tell you how I get on any stage I want, how I get thousands of eye balls on my business, and how I get free news coverage anytime I want it. Is it okay if I over-deliver? ;)

We are in the marketing phase, and our goal is to get to the movement phase ($100k+ a month). To do this, we will need a lot of social proof while maximizing our audience and creating a real impact.

When starting from ground zero and not having a zillion dollars for Facebook ads, I go to the Guinness World Record website where there are hundreds of records that are incredibly easy to break. (I've broken four of them with no investment.)

You might say, "Kolton, that's great, but how is breaking the world's largest checkers record going to help my sandwich shop or social media agency?"

Great question! Okay, find a record you think you can break, announce it on Facebook, and start getting some attention. Once you have some interest online, it's time to pick up the phone and start calling news agencies and letting them know you are breaking a world record, donating a portion of proceeds to charity, and you'd like to give them an exclusive story.

Are your wheels turning yet? Because yes, it is that simple. You can and should contact every news agency and radio station to give them an "exclusive." You now have news coverage where you can talk about your event, why you are giving back, and about the company doing it.

You now have tons of social proof, PR, testimonials, and most importantly a *ton* of eyeballs on you without much (if any) investment.

This simple method is what got me out of homelessness to making $70k at my first event, "The World's Largest Super Soaker Battle." I ended up getting tons of new coverage, raised money for veterans, and partnered with companies like Hasbro, Nestle, Vita Coco, Subaru, Redbull, General Motors, and many more.

This method can be modified and replicated over and over, I've used variations to get on stage with Russell Brunson, Snoop Dogg, 50 Cent, the Dallas Cowboys, and many more.

I've used this leverage to get me in a meeting with the one and only James Smiley, and we have since created an amazing business that is impacting lives around the world.

If your brain hasn't exploded yet, hopefully it will as I get to my final core principle: MOVEMENT. The movement phase is how you go from $100k a month to over $1 million a month.

Movement can be defined as "a group of people working together to advance their shared political, social, or artistic ideas." That's almost scary, isn't it? This movement can be and has been used for both good and evil.

I'm assuming we are all good people, so it will be used for good. A movement is where we take the marketing we have done and get people behind it.

For example, think of ClickFunnels. Right when they were doing $100k+ a month, they shifted to creating a movement. This is where you get people to identify with your brand. ClickFunnels uses the term "funnel hackers."

In the movement phase, people are using your brand in their profile pictures and wearing your swag every day to the point where it drives everyone crazy. This is the part where people will even tattoo your logo on their body. Yes, I've seen it, and no, it's not something I recommend, but you see what I'm saying.

When you look at all the heavy hitters like Gary V, Russell Brunson, Tony Robbins, and many others, you'll see it doesn't matter what they sell. The moment they put something on the market, everyone goes absolutely nuts. Everyone buys their stuff because they've created a movement.

A movement is also important when things go wrong. Ups and downs happen in business, and when you have a movement, you are essentially creating armor for your business.

When something goes wrong with any of the above-mentioned, it's like everyone locks arms to ride out the storm together. That's how you keep your business through tough times.

This is the exact phase I had personally messed up with my private military company that I scaled to seven figures. Long story short, there was a temporary government freeze on jobs, so my company could not train veterans for jobs that no longer existed.

I was focusing on marketing instead of focusing on creating a movement, so when this storm came down on my business, it's like I turned around and everyone was gone. I was alone when news agencies were at my door falsely calling me a scammer.

Notice at the beginning I said "temporary" freeze on jobs. What would have been different if I had focused on creating a movement and that government freeze happened? We would have all locked arms and weathered the storm together because, just like any storm, it will eventually go away, and the sun will come out again.

To recap, this is the reason I put a monetary value on my three core principles. In some cases it will vary, but in my experience it's pretty on point.

Mindset: $0–$10k/mo
Marketing $10k–$100k/mo
Movement $100k+/mo

These principles took me from homeless to millionaire, and I promise it can do the exact same for you. I will never forget where I came from, and it was not long ago I was in a shelter with nothing but a dream and the willpower to change my current situation. And that's all *you* need.

I like to tell people that if you have an internet connection and a pulse, you can make money online.

I hope you enjoyed this, and if you ever need any help or want to talk with me about where you currently are in your business, feel free to reach out to me on just about any social media platform.

ABOUT KOLTON KROTTINGER

Krottinger is a decorated U.S. Navy veteran, two-time World Record holder, Amazon best-selling author, ClickFunnels 2 Comma Club member, and Dream Car winner. From homeless to millionaire, Kolton Krottinger impacts thousands of lives across the globe and has helped hundreds of businesses turn profitable.

kolton@krottinger.com
krottinger.com

NOTES

5 STEP VIDEO AND SOCIAL MEDIA METHOD WE USE TO GET UNLIMITED HIGH-TICKET TRAFFIC (WORKS EVEN IF YOU'RE A SOLOPRENEUR)

by Tracey Wong

Video is on an upward trajectory. Within the next five years, mobile video will increase by 870% of what it is right now. Imagine how many hours of video are already online and increase that by 870%. That's huge!

Instead of posting something on social media that only has text and images, if you just replace that with a video, you'll have a 1200% increase in social shares on average.

The two biggest platforms right now are Facebook and YouTube. There are 2 billion people on Facebook and 1.5 billion people on YouTube. Mark Zuckerberg says that Facebook will probably be 100% video in 5 years. So if you're not on video or you're not getting on video, you're going to be left far behind. You need to be creating video content.

I've been helping James Smiley by increasing his reach through video. One thing we've been working on is a video lead funnel with three parts. Instead of using a website to do this, we've just been using social media.

Going from a video to PM/DM to getting someone on the phone is the fastest way to the cash.

We posted a video natively on Facebook and YouTube for James on Tuesday, and within 30 minutes we were getting reactions. Someone saw the video on Tuesday, bought a ticket on Wednesday, and came to the mastermind on Thursday. That's how effective video can be.

James receives 2 to 5 leads per video, closing about 50% of them. The two packages he sells are between $5K and $15K, and he's spending zero on ad spend, which is pretty incredible.

My first case study I want to tell you about is actually one of my side businesses and is how I was able to get free client acquisition. It was something I was doing in my spare time because I love health and fitness. By putting up some videos on my page where I only had 200 likes, I was able to extract 15 coaching clients. That's unbelievable.

My second case study is with a traditional funnel using the power of one good video. We cut a video down to 8 minutes and aggregated all the testimonials. We edited the video 3 or 4 times to make sure that it had the right script. This testimony highlight reel reached a diverse demographic and allowed James to grow a business to 6 figures in 2.5 months with zero ad spend.

The third case study is a viral video on a political Facebook page that had 5,000 people. We created a way to film and edit the video where we knew it would capture people completely and they would watch it all the way through. This one video reached 2.6 million people with 1.4 million views in only 13 days. The page got 12,000 new page likes with zero ad spend.

This is my video secret.

The reason why a lot of sales funnels aren't working is because people are not analyzing the video. Why do videos autoplay? Because they draw you in at the beginning. So the video is not just one component in the sales funnel. It *is* the funnel.

We've all been made to think that the video is just a tiny little portion of it when it's actually the key part. People watch the video even before they pay attention the headline.

Video isn't stagnant; it's a story. So, instead of it being one box, it's broken up into segments.

When you go to the movies and you watch a movie with a crappy ending, do you ever think that they didn't have good equipment? No, you think the story sucked. You think that the person who wrote it didn't do a good job with the story.

Even though we're doing these video sales letters, this is basically a short form of a story. There's the beginning, the middle, and the end.

Tony Robbins says that you need emotion, and once you have the emotion, it will put you to a place where you get into motion. We need some type of emotion to get people to do something in motion. But before you get to do that, you need to get their attention.

You have 10 seconds to get people's attention. There are studies that show that you need to capture people's attention within 6 to 9 seconds. Attention spans are getting shorter and shorter.

Here's how you get attention.

If you're a lady, your power is in your looks. I used to be a makeup artist in LA for several years, so I know the power of putting a woman in a makeup chair, transforming her, and then putting her back into the world. Her new looks created a compelling and completely different reaction.

For men, it's not about your looks, it's about being interesting. Gary Vaynerchuk says you either have to be pretty, funny, or extremely talented. If you can get people's attention, you bridge them to the next stage.

The next part is emotion. This is what I call "uncovering the epiphany."

The way to have someone change their mind is by telling them a story. You take them from where they were at the beginning and then transfer them to a place where they agree with you. You have to speak to people's hearts.

One very good example is Steve Jobs. When he came out with the iPhone, everyone was using the Blackberry. But then they saw what the iPhone did, it changed their minds. It created a desire, an epiphany. Steve Jobs uncovered an epiphany, and he was so good at it that he took them to an emotional state, and then he bridged them to a state where they got into motion. When you get people to the state of motion, it's like destiny is calling them.

All of us have a desire for something greater. There's a void inside of us, and we want to be part of something that's bigger than ourselves. Use video to tell a story that reaches us emotionally and causes us to get into motion.

ABOUT TRACEY WONG

Tracey is a photographer, filmmaker, and one of the most highly sought-after social media strategists with various 7 and 8-figure entrepreneur clients such as Grant Cardone, Brendon Burchard, and Ryan Moran.

Her videos have helped entrepreneurs generate multi-6-figure incomes and are viewed by millions of people every week.

Other top-rated digital marketing clients include James Smiley, Steve Larsen, Josh Forti, and JR Rivas.

Tracey is a USC grad and majored in International Relations.

tracey@theimagetalks.com
traceywong.media

NOTES

NOTES

SEXY FADES WHILE STEADY PAYS

by William Cheverie

"SEX SELLS!"

It's been the battle cry of advertising campaigns since Ford saw a significant jump in sales by placing a model in the ad with the fledgling Mustang.

But now, sexy has given way to stories, and to gain influence and earn significant online income those stories had better be steady.

My photo is here so it's easy to see that I am, shall we say a mature gentleman. My sexy may have long since faded, but it's been the steady and consistent daily activities and step-by-step process that I methodically practice and teach that has led to almost five million dollars in online commissions and a "steady" five-figure monthly residual income for my family as well as my students.

"DIGITAL DOMINANCE REQUIRES A DAILY BLUEPRINT"

Earlier in my life, I owned a couple of pizza restaurants. For the first year, they hemorrhaged money. Even though sales were great, and people loved the food, I was working 70 hours a week for minimum wage. That was not the plan.

As I sat pouring over the weekly numbers trying to figure out why I wasn't being profitable, an epiphany hit me that would change my business mindset for the rest of my life.

Don't think weekly, think daily! Suddenly, everything changed. I made a daily sheet of all costs and income and started tracking how, what, and where the money and time was coming in and going out.

107

The final part of the puzzle came a few weeks later but was in front of me the whole time. You see, in the food business, freshness counts. It was crucial to have fresh-baked sub rolls from the bakery every morning, so the last thing we did everyday was ensure tomorrow's success by ordering those sub rolls. Eureka!

Begin every day with an action plan and end each day with a plan for tomorrow. Don't wake up wondering what to do today. Already have that plan in place and watch what a difference it makes. Profits soared, and I started working far less hours for a lot more money.

Later, as I transitioned into the online world, I defined this process even further and developed a unique hybrid system of online marketing whereby short bursts of focused activity could allow myself and those I teach make more money in less time allowing more time for family, activities, self, and fun. What does this blueprint look like? Well, in actuality it's fairly simple.

"SHORT DAILY BURSTS OF MISSION-DRIVEN ACTIVITY"

If the title were longer, the second part would read, "NOT hours of online time-wasting bull shit."

Realize that business needs new customers to survive, and the latest stats show there is over a 90% chance those customers are on social media. Knowing this means you need to divide your time into precise increments and sit down with a plan of attack. This plan is your blueprint and includes contacting people on your Dream 100 list, posting valuable content in groups, different social media apps, and your personal timeline, making new contacts and connections, and then following up with seeds already planted or eliminating deadwood. Keeping detailed notes is crucial to this blueprint process.

Short bursts means exactly that. Bursts are short bouts of intense mission-driven energy. Each 15-minute burst must be mission-driven to each assignment in the above blueprint. Realistically, a person can't maintain that intensity for long periods, so the strategy is to divide your time into one-hour blocks and then take a break—change your state and shift attention—A.K.A. get away from the computer.

"Date the Strategy but Marry the Vision"

The world of online marketing and influence changes daily. Models change, apps change, and we all know that certainly algorithms constantly change. While you'll be adapting and competing daily, be flexible in your strategies but unwavering with your vision.

Review: "Rules and Mindset"

Before you begin, there are three important principals to understand.

#1- Is to have fun. Why else would we choose to do this daily? Plus passion and energy communicates, and there is a special, contagious magnet from those having fun in what they're doing.

#2- Be customer-centric or align yourself with a client or service that is because that is what creates authentic, residual income.

#3- Be of the mindset that allowing my customer to go to the competition is to do them a disservice. Your posture must exude that you have the best solution they need.

Every successful entrepreneur knows there may be hacks, but there are no shortcuts. Persistence and perseverance will defeat talent every time.

Sexy fades and history teaches us there is no substitute for experience.

When you're trying to climb to the top of mountain, choose a guide who's already scaled it.

ABOUT WILLIAM CHEVERIE

Upon graduation, William served in the Army where he learned the importance of discipline and the ability to problem-solve by adapting to change quickly.

After his service, William was drawn to becoming an entrepreneur, and then started and sold several successful restaurants, real estate endeavors, and other businesses.

That success quickly turned into a passion for helping other entrepreneurs find a new level of success using innovative marketing and branding strategies.

William coached entrepreneurs his methods to find untapped potential within themselves as well as new revenue sources within their businesses.

Seeing a need for his unique marketing techniques in other niches, he entered the field of affiliate marketing where he is credited as the first person to successfully develop a hybrid marketing system that helps marketers earn higher commissions with greater retention. Having received millions in commissions, William now teaches and mentors others in marketing, branding, and online influence. His system helps anyone in the field of marketing explore greater revenue possibilities.

William is a husband, father and grandfather. He has enjoyed a lifetime of success in business, fitness, and helping others reach their goals.

info@williamcheverie.com
williamcheverie.com

NOTES

NOTES

"AUTHORING" INFLUENCE

by Aaron Janda

I t was a couple weeks before Christmas. The air was brisk, and everyone was dressed to the nines. It was that time of year again, giving and receiving gifts, enjoying time with friends and family, and some of the best social events in the city. I stepped outside onto the rooftop overlooking the city with utter amazement as to how my life had changed in just a few short months. I found myself at the top of a corporate building in a penthouse suite, at an invite-only party with CEOs, heads of major corporations, multi-millionaires, influencers, political figures and the one man who was able to get me there.

Just a couple of months before the party, my newly published book, *My $100 Dollar Project* had made it into the hands of that one man, a very prominent and influential person, the president and CEO of a major bank within the city. The book was about a simple project I did teaching people how to turn $100 into a $1000 and beyond by applying ROI principles. I wrote it because I wanted to inspire the next generation into business and change their perspectives on money.

I had met this CEO and his assistant briefly at a business event but didn't think much about the encounter until a couple of days later when I received a phone call from the assistant:

"Hello, is this Aaron Janda?"

"Yes, it is."

"Hello, we spoke briefly the other day. Well, my boss got ahold of your book, and he loved it! He was wondering if you would meet him for lunch. He would love to sit down with you and get to know you a bit more."

Very quickly I realized that it wasn't what I "knew" about business, investing, or how much money I made that had created this amazing connection and friendship. *It was my unique story that he read about it in my book.* Then, organically, that friendship opened new doors, created new connections, and manifested new opportunities. Ironically, the blessings that came out of that connection were truly not based on *what* I knew but *who* I knew, and that "who" had found me through my book.

But here's the thing. Writing a book that helped other people and opened doors for me isn't something only I can do. *Every person reading these words has a book inside them*! Everyone has had unique life experiences which means they have something extremely special to share with the world. Whether someone has been homeless or drives a Lamborghini, everyone has had their share of struggles and successes, dark times and good times, low points and high points! And from those experiences, people have learned valuable lessons. And what they learn not only has the power to change their own life, but influence others lives as well!

This statistic has made me passionate about inspiring people to share their own stories! Over 84% of people have thought about or have wanted to write a book, yet less than 5% actually do! Think of all the wisdom and knowledge other people miss out on because those who should write books never do! I want to help change that statistic.

How different would your life be if you wrote your own book? How many lives would be changed and inspired by hearing your story? What doors of opportunity would open because you've accomplished something most people never do? It's hard to know unless you actually do. People need to hear what you have to say! I would never have inspired the people I had, or been granted access to the places, people and experiences in my life if I had not put myself out there to publish my own book.

Whether you are a single mom that has accomplished something great and wants to share it with the world or a corporate level executive who wants to set yourself apart, authoring your story — sharing your experience, your expertise, or your accomplishments — will impact people's lives. And it will change your life in the process! It will widen your current circle of influence, establish you as an authority in your space, and take you to places you could not have ever imagined. I've been through the process and have experienced the benefits of publishing a book. Now I want to challenge, encourage, and coach you through a program that will take you all the way from brainstorming your book to holding a finished copy in your hands. After that, the sky's the limit on who you can influence and how that influence can change your life.

I will be screening a limited group for my next "Done With You" program. If you would like more information contact me to schedule your screening call.

ABOUT AARON JANDA

Aaron Janda is among a new generation of authors, speakers, and entrepreneurs. Aaron authored his first book *My $100 Dollar Project,* a book that inspires readers to take $100 and multiply it into $1000 and beyond. Aaron is a successful business owner and influencer who has created multiple streams of income for his family and is helping empower others to do the same.

info@aaronjanda.com
aaronjanda.com

NOTES

NOTES

SUCCESS WITHOUT SYSTEMS

by April Zarling

People tell me all the time they have a successful business without any systems. Initially, I had no idea what their fate would be but soon learned that to be successful as a business owner or entrepreneur, you must have systems. I know this now because I started without any systems in place and learned the hard way.

We all live in an era where everyone has immediate access to information online, "experts" at their fingertips, and a never-ending display of ads everywhere we go. My biggest struggle as an entrepreneur was trying to figure out which of those experts I could trust and to weed through the dishonesty and the "fake it till you make its." Now, don't get me wrong, I believe every entrepreneur needs to display a level of confidence because we all start at the bottom and work our way up, but I believe also displaying a level of honesty with your prospective customers will increase your potential for success.

On our path to success, we all need to understand our limitations and areas for growth. I see many entrepreneurs struggling to figure out their limitations and ultimately fail because they aren't willing to accept their weaknesses and learn from them. I got to a point in my business where I couldn't research anymore and needed to find mentors that could help me with specific areas of growth that I was facing. I spent several months watching the mentors within my circle and learning from them. I didn't act quickly, and I didn't just hand over money to random people that persuaded me. I think a large majority of entrepreneurs can act on emotions rather than logic, and it can get them in a bind. I've also chosen mentors that were of no help to me, but I recognized that, accepted my losses, and moved on to someone that would get me to where I needed to be.

Understanding your limitations is a difficult process, but as long as you accept responsibility and work toward your goal, you will be able to understand what you're good at and what you need to outsource to become successful in the online space.

Outsourcing and recognizing when you can be more productive by doing so is a large part of being an entrepreneur. Many successful entrepreneurs have most likely been through this phase and understand the process, but a few years ago I didn't, nor was I willing to, accept that I could not do it all. I can also say that I was not successful until I was willing to outsource. At first, it's hard to accept that you have to spend money to make money, especially when you're not making any money. I look at who everyone else is recommending and make an ongoing list as I come across people's names, services, and recommendations so that I can come back to it when I need help from another person or business. I will also search that person's name across various Facebook groups to see what additional information comes up, good or bad, to make my decision. What worked well for me was mapping out my entire day-to-day processes from start to finish as if I were going to train another person. I then chose which of those areas I didn't like doing, took too much time, or I wasn't good at, and found other people that could do the job, which pushed my business to the next level.

Taking your business to the next level can be one of the most challenging times in your life. Four key things have led to exponential growth in my business: Finding the right mentor and firing those that aren't, exploring and accepting my limitations, outsourcing when I could no longer do it all, and setting up systems to bring everything together. I struggled for months trying to weed my way through, managing and implementing absolutely every part of my business, and having zero systems in place. I woke up one day and realized that I wasn't getting anywhere. I wasn't leveraging anything, and I was just spinning my wheels like every other JOB prior to becoming an entrepreneur. I strive every day to encourage other entrepreneurs in the info space to take this advice, move forward, and let go of the things that are holding them back. Being an entrepreneur has been a rollercoaster ride for me, but understanding and going along for the ride will put any entrepreneur steps ahead of their competition by just accepting and letting go of 100% control.

ABOUT APRIL ZARLING

April Zarling is an entrepreneur and information product inventor who helps independent insurance adjusters break into the industry through innovative systems and mentorship.

Before starting in the information product space, she started out in the workforce as a Registered Nurse and moved on to be an Insurance Adjuster. After realizing that there was a need for better mentorship and training of new adjusters, she created an information course and mentorship program to fill the gap, which in turn has allowed adjusters from every walk of life become successful in the industry.

April has successfully trained and mentored many individuals into the insurance adjusting world by giving her students information and techniques that others aren't using or willing to share. One of her biggest strengths is teaching them how to leverage the Internet and create systems to ensure their success.

April enjoys the outdoors where she lives in Colorado with her husband and two kids. Her hobbies include traveling, photography, exercise, reading, and creating new and innovative business opportunities.

NOTES

BREAKING THE CHAINS OF BRICK AND MORTAR FOR THE FREEDOM OF ONLINE BUSINESS

by Baldeep Chawla

B uilding brick and mortar businesses with over 15 locations, 3 franchise brands, 250 employees, with 7-figure revenues is a lot to accomplish in 6 years. It comes with its challenges including 7-figure rent, payroll, taxes, utilities, and more importantly, time. Time away from family and loved ones to build your "dream" does not necessarily afford a great lifestyle. Remember the old saying, "It can take 2 to 3 years for your business to become profitable". It makes sense. When you lease a storefront location for your business, you are immediately cashflow negative. You must deal with security deposits for your lease, construction and buildout costs, ongoing rent until the location is ready, and hiring and training employees as well as marketing your business. And you must deal with all of this before you've had the chance to even open the doors to generate revenue. It's no wonder that most small businesses fail within the first five years, it's an uphill battle, and you need to be ready for war. You learn from your mistakes, but make enough of them, and your business may not be around for the next one.

There are tremendous benefits to transitioning to an online business. You can get started with minimal overhead and generate revenue before spending thousands of dollars. Never before have we been able to prove a concept before building a business. The freedom to spend more time with your family while building your dream is life-changing. How do you successfully transition into a business that affords true freedom like marketing consulting? Let's break it down in four simple steps: Identify, Prospect, Offer, Delivery.

Identify: There are three criteria to look for in this step.

- Do you like them?

- Can you help them?

- Are they spending money?

The first criteria should be obvious; you need to like who you serve. Imagine spending all day talking to potential clients you can't stand? It will cause you to quickly get discouraged and give up. Make a list of industries and types of customers you would absolutely love speaking with. Then make sure you can help them. What can you do to help them reach their goals? Are you able to provide them with more customers? Design a better website for them? Help them convert more sales? It is important to zero in on how you can best serve your ideal client. Finally, they must be spending money on growing their business. Never try to convince a business that they should be investing in their growth.

Prospect: Getting in front of your potential client is crucial to your success. The biggest mistake many business owners make is to think they can just put up a sign and expect people to walk in. The same is true for online businesses. There are multiple ways to reach out to your market. Below are just a few.

1. Cold email and cold calling

2. LinkedIn

3. Facebook Ads

4. Direct mail

5. YouTube

Find the method that works best for you, and then step on the gas and generate consistent client opportunities.

Offer: "Ask and you shall receive." Realistically, if you are having conversations with potential clients and you do not ask for the sale, there will never be one. Keep in mind that the first part of your conversation should not be focused on the sale. Build a process for ultimately making the offer. Ask questions about their business and learn about their needs, goals, desires, and pain points. It's crucial to listen as the answers they are giving you are the keys you need to unlock the door to their desired outcome. How can you best serve their needs? When you ask the right questions and your service is a solution to their problem, the offer becomes a simple transaction based on the value you can provide.

Delivery: Your client just paid you money! Now, it's time to make good on your offer. The most important part of this step is communication. Keeping an open line of communication with your client is key to long-term retention and referrals. Even if you are not the one fulfilling on the delivery (for example if you contracted out the work to a freelancer or white label company), make sure to set and properly manage expectations in the relationship for long term success.

There are a lot of fancy methods you can use to build your online business. As entrepreneurs, it is easy to get lost in the pursuit of the next best thing. Beware of Shiny Object Syndrome. I encourage you to keep it simple and focus on these four steps, and then you can build a successful business focused on helping others so you can achieve your dreams.

ABOUT BALDEEP CHAWLA

Baldeep is no stranger to the idea of jumping off the cliff and building an airplane on the way down. His foundation at an early age was built within an entrepreneurial family that taught him to never comprise his time and freedom for a 9-5. He purchased his first brick and mortar franchise business in 2009 and never looked back—kicking off the start of his entrepreneurial journey. Within five years at the franchise, he was successfully operating 15 locations in 5 states from New York to California with an annual revenue in excess of $3.4 M. In that same time frame, Baldeep continued to explore and to expand other opportunities both in and out of the franchise arena. He purchased and grew an Area Development (Master Franchise) from 9 locations to 40 (77.5% growth) in 3 years producing $5.0 M in gross revenue. To further diversify his portfolio, he purchased 2 other franchise concepts during this timeframe.

In 2015, Baldeep decided to settle down when he married his beautiful wife and started to build a family while building a mindset around a business model that allowed him the freedom to build a business online. Understanding fast-paced market changes, Baldeep decided to comfortably make his latest leap into the marketing and advertising world. As a seasoned business mogul, this allowed Baldeep to take his range of skills and business craftsmanship that ventured into a web-based marketing firm. Today, similar to his previous jumps, he is yet again on the verge of building two multi-million dollar successes simultaneously, but this time on his own terms without the restriction of brick and mortar, allowing him a lifestyle that provides freedom, time, and resources for his wife and family.

bchawla@clearskylocal.com
clearskylocal.com

NOTES

NOTES

HOW TO CREATE HIGH-CONVERTING SALES COPY WITHOUT KNOWING ANYTHING ABOUT SALES

by Ed Bordi

It's really easy to create high-converting sales scripts, emails, videos, and web copy from scratch with this simple trick I learned about a decade ago—even without knowing anything about sales, human psychology or persuasion.

But first, a story to help illustrate.

I think I do an okay job dressing myself, but it usually takes two or three tries before my wife approves my ensemble. And that's with her coaching me through the entire selection process. Here's how it usually goes: I strut across the room feeling good but apparently looking bad. Without words, her expression says it all. I know what she's thinking. "Seriously?"

I do an about-face and try again.

This makes gift-buying stressful. I want her to love the outfits I buy, but there's no chance of that happening with my horrendous eye for fashion. I needed a solution and I found one.

The mannequin.

I walk into the store, find the best dressed mannequin, and buy everything it's wearing, including shoes and jewelry. This trick makes gift-buying easy. As long as I know my wife's sizes and favorite shops, the whole process takes minutes.

Now, every time I buy her an outfit, she absolutely loves it but is puzzled. I can see her wheels spinning, wondering how in the world I pulled off that incredible feat.

Maybe you're wondering what all this has to do with you and sales. I'm getting to the point. I promise.

You know who puts together those mannequins? Professional stylists. They know how to coordinate colors, patterns, and styles. They know trends. They know how to accessorize with jewelry and shoes and belts.

Those mannequins look amazing!

I don't need to know anything; I just leverage their expertise. And as a consequence of doing this for years, I ended up learning a thing or two about fashion. I'm no longer horrendous, just slightly unpleasant.

Okay, now to the point of the story.

When I write sales copy, I use my "mannequin" technique.

Even with my below average copywriting skills, I'm able to produce emails, sales letters, advertisements, and other marketing materials that deliver excellent results—conversion rates on par with the professionals.

Here's how I do it.

I'm always on the lookout for great copy—junk mail, email, websites, and advertisements. If they work on me, I save them to my swipe file.

Swipe file—(noun): a collection of sales, advertising and marketing materials used as inspiration for new projects.

If I see an email subject line that makes me click—I save it.

If I see an ad that makes me click—I save it.

If I read a sales letter that convinces me to buy—I save it.

Over the years, I've amassed a giant collection of copy I reference all of the time for ideas; it's my mannequin. Whenever I need a little inspiration, I crack it open.

In the words of Mark Twain, "There is no such thing as a new idea. It is impossible. We simply take a lot of old ideas and put them into a sort of mental kaleidoscope. We give them a turn and they make new and curious combinations. They are the same old pieces of colored glass that have been in use through all the ages."

This is the same reason you don't see many new scripts from Hollywood. Most movies are remakes of the classics.

It's also how you can compete with major brands and big guru budgets able to pay 5 and 6 figures to a copywriter.

Use the "mannequin" technique to make a ton of money while you learn.

And I definitely recommend you learn. Devote time to cultivating your copywriting prowess. You'll be glad you did. Many have said (and I agree), it's the single most important skill you can possess as an entrepreneur.

It's how you create money with words.

Make it a priority. Go learn the art and science of copywriting!

It's a science, because there are proven psychological triggers that move people to action—words, ideas, and even colors. Countless formulas have been developed by copywriting legends that break down the steps into a repeatable process.

It's an art because the more you do it, the better you get. I can attest to that. I still use my swipe file but not as often. Practice has made it come a little bit easier. When I first started writing, I would copy, word for word, sales letters written by Dan Kennedy, Gary Halbert, John Carlton, and others. This exercise helped me internalize their style and flow so that when I wrote my own copy, it had the same feel.

There you go. Now you know how to become an amazing copywriter, make a bunch of money and buy the perfect gift.

There you go. Now you know how to become an amazing copywriter, make a bunch of money—and buy the perfect gift.

ABOUT ED BORDI

Edward Bordi is a sought-after and respected digital marketer, award-winning software / technology architect and business coach.

His systems and guidance have enabled companies in diverse industries to accelerated growth and operational savings ≈ $300 million.

Edward has worked closely with and counseled 50+ C-suite professionals. His insightful ideas, simple solutions and step-by-step approach has quickly made him one of the most in-demand advisors for entrepreneurs and executives.

He served several large enterprises including Verizon, Yahoo and Computer Associates, plus hundreds of solopreneurs, small to medium-sized businesses and non-profits.

He authored 200+ tech / marketing articles, 2 books, mentored elite young talent from around the country, spoke on stage to Internet Millionaires and appeared on Sales Funnel Radio.

Edward studied business / marketing / technology in the Executive Masters in Technology Management (EMTM) program at Wharton and the University of Pennsylvania's school of Engineering. He holds a bachelor's degree in Computer Science from Rowan University and has multiple certifications, including a Lean Six Sigma green belt.

After three decades of using, refining and teaching marketing and technology, he's taking his experience, connections and insider knowledge of winning business strategies and bringing them to you.

Want to work with Edward? Visit www.edwardbordi.com

ed@1easyplan.com
edwardbordi.com

NOTES

NOTES

THE PROVEN FORMULA TO CRUSH IT ON INSTAGRAM

by Håkon Østerberg

Back in the day, I stumbled across Instagram while I was trying to get more exposure and traffic to my website. Since then, Instagram has truly changed my business and my life. What makes Instagram so special is that with zero experience or followers, you can immediately reach millions and turning those people into loyal fans and costumers if you do it right.

Instagram recently passed 1 billion monthly users and the engagement levels are still sky-high compared to other platforms. With 80% of pages following a business page on Instagram, it confirms the great business opportunity that marketers can take advantage off.

Instagram is a photo and video-sharing platform where the content itself is key to successfully master the platform. You can do the world's best growth strategies, but unless you have good quality content or something interesting to showcase, people will not follow you. They may get into your page, but not go and press that magic "follow button." You have around one to three seconds to capture potential followers' attention on Instagram. That means that you need to impress them with unique consistent quality content to get their attention. When it comes to content creating, it is important to stand out by having sharp high-resolution photos, proper lighting, and a consistent style.

Consistently posting is one of the most overlooked strategies when it comes to success on Instagram. If you look at the most successful pages on Instagram, they all post consistent and relevant content. With Instagram's algorithmic timeline, consistency is a key element to getting your posts seen and appearing at the top of the feed. If your posts are shared on a regular basis and pick up good engagement, then Instagram's algorithm places your posts at the top of your followers' feeds and increases your exposure.

As mentioned, one of the key ways to grow your Instagram following is to post high-quality content consistently to get your followers more engaged. The question is how do you know what content your followers want? How do you get them to engage with you? And how do you get your content out to reach thousands of people daily? It all comes down to putting in the extra work behind the curtains and doing proper market research. Find out what content your target market already engages with, what captions are being used, and how the pages interact with their fans on IGTV, Instagram Stories, and livestreams. Does a certain type of content get more impressions or engagement? Post more of those images or videos and see if your followers continue to like and engage more with them.

Your content is what keeps people following your page and engaging with it, but hashtags are the key to build up your exposure and get new people into your page. Instagram is built around hashtags, and it is the most effective way to get your content out to the people that are not already following your page. The goal is to rank in the top post under those hashtags, and then expose your content to a large and targeted audience.

Most people do one of two things when selecting hashtags. They either target hashtags that are way too big, which results in barely any followers because they can't rank, or they target hashtags that are way too small, so that even if they do rank, nobody sees the content. And even if the hashtags have millions of posts under it, you can rank in them if you use a strategy called hashtag stacking. Stacking is simple, and you stack the hashtags in order by competition. The stack contains a total of 30 hashtags, with 10 small, 10 medium, and 10 large ones. When you combine these together, it's easier to rank. By using market research and finding the perfect set of hashtags, you can get your content out to thousands without having a large following.

Instagram is a social platform, and to be able to succeed, you need to create a network in your niche. By collaborating with others, you can be able to both provide value to a new audience and grow faster together. If you create your own network in your niche, it can turn out to be more powerful and valuable than the page itself. If you have the budget, influencer marketing is still very underpriced, and a great opportunity to gain massive exposure for your brand.

While Instagram started as a photo-sharing network, it has grown beyond only photos. To be able to grow and build up your awareness on Instagram, you need to utilize all features: videos, live videos, IGTV, and Stories. This is a great way to build up your brand, show behind the scenes content, and connect with your audience.

ABOUT HÅKON ØSTERBERG

The Internet has made it possible for anyone that puts in the work to build both their influence and income. With zero experience or followers, you can immediately reach millions on Instagram and turn those people into loyal fans and customers if you do it right. This differentiates the Instagram platform from other platforms and gives people who are starting out or want to scale their business an incredible opportunity.

The strategies I have used to build up a huge and loyal audience of over 200,000 people with a network of 2 million people on Instagram comes down to four main pillars: content, consistency, market research, and networking. To succeed on Instagram, you need to know your niche, what people are posting, the times they post, how often they post, what hashtags they use, and how they engage with their audience. The next step is to put out good quality content on a consistent basis and find people to do collaborations with in your niche.

These are the exact same strategies that I have used to grow my pages to over 200,000 followers on Instagram and help dozens of others business build up their influence and income from Instagram.

hakon@hakonosterberg.com
hakonosterberg.com

NOTES

NOTES

B2B PODCASTING
THE MOST POWERFUL SALES
TOOL YOU CAN CREATE

by Jason Croft

With the rise in popularity of podcasting and creating video content on YouTube, entrepreneurs and sales pros are buying into the concept that these channels are important.

The problem is, most are only seeing it through the lens of "content marketing" and "building a personal brand" over time. Creating your own original content will certainly lead to those outcomes, but those are secondary in comparison to the immediate sales channel results they can provide.

Podcasting is the greatest cold outreach tool there is for sales. I learned this completely by accident.

With my first show, Startup Dallas, I decided to have a video interview show that posted on YouTube along with a podcast version up on iTunes. I interviewed top CEOs, startup founders, and sales and marketing professionals in the Dallas startup scene. We had a three-camera shoot set up in the studios of the production company I worked for at the time.

Like most people starting a podcast or producing video content like this, I did it as a form of content marketing. I had recently discovered the amazing startup scene in the Dallas area, and I wanted a way to stand out, contribute, and hopefully start building a client base of folks in the community.

The show succeeded in three ways:

1. It got me a "seat at the table" in the startup community immediately. By shining a spotlight on its members, this group invited me in and wanted me to participate in events all over town.

2. It showed me the power of having a platform. I realized very quickly that practically no one says "no" when invited to be on the show. This was a powerful realization that I'll expand on more in a bit.

3. It grew my network at an exponential rate. I was creating great relationships with guests I had on my show, cultivating them further offline, and those folks introduced me to more people they felt I should know. And with the audience of the show, more people reached out just to connect.

I also quite accidentally realized that I loved doing this. I had never put myself in front of the camera to any degree, despite having been behind the camera for 20+ years at the time. And though I certainly wasn't great right away, I fell in love with it, which kept me doing it, which led to those benefits above.

I did 81 episodes of Startup Dallas, and when I left that production company, I knew I had to start a show of my own.

So, what I realized as I was starting The Jason Croft Show was the fact that no ever refused to be on that first show.

I realized what a powerful sales tool a podcast can be. Why not invite my ideal prospects on the show? Why not use the show to meet amazing people I find online and learn from them?

I coach my clients on this all the time. Running a non-profit? Start a show about your cause and invite the people on whom you hope will donate. Do you sell for a SaaS company and just can't get a meeting with the CTO? Have him or her on your show discussing the problems for which your software provides solutions.

I know you may be thinking that you've never interviewed anyone. And maybe the idea of starting and running your own show is massively overwhelming. There are a lot of moving parts to get set up in the beginning, but so much of that can be outsourced. And once you get set up and have your process down, the interviews themselves are simply conversations. In fact, you can structure much of your conversation around the same questions you'd normally ask a prospect on a sales call.

And even though you may be interviewing most of your guests in the hopes that they become clients (or introduce you clients), you're still leading with value. By having them on your show, you're giving that guest a chance to stand in a spotlight and build their credibility with their following and client base.

Please don't over-complicate this or talk yourself out of it based on having never done it. Start simple with just audio and by interviewing your friends. Having a video aspect to your show is great. Audio-only podcasts, though, are certainly powerful enough to achieve what I'm describing here. Heck, you can even accomplish similar goals with a written blog, though the relationship that gets developed isn't always as cemented.

I hope you've had an "aha" moment or two with this and realize what an amazing sales tool a show can be. Now, just start!

ABOUT JASON CROFT

Jason Croft is a media strategist with a specialty in corporate podcast creation and video marketing.

With his company, Croft Media, he creates B2B Sales Funnel Podcasts for clients and Authority Interview Videos for consultants and other solopreneurs.

He is now hosting and running a business video show and podcast, The Jason Croft Show. With it, Croft takes the same approach of in-depth interviewing of his guests that he's become known for and adds a twist of fun—setting each episode in a moving vehicle and finding out what really drives them.

He is also the host of Strategy + Action, a thriving Meetup in Dallas, TX bringing entrepreneurs and tech enthusiasts together every week.

Jason loves his amazing wife and three boys, has a blast traveling around the world, and often gets too close to exotic animals. He's been on icebergs and mountains, kissed and wrestled with black bears (pictures upon request), and even swam with a shark (not by choice!).

jason@croftmediaco.com
croftmediaco.com

NOTES

NOTES

ORGANICALLY GROWING YOUR BUSINESS WITH A SMALL BUDGET

by Javier Lozano, Jr

Today's consumer or business tends to listen to the loudest people on social media, blogs, vlogs, podcasts, and other media outlets.

But, they have also developed a keen ear (and eye) for knowing which people are blowing smoke.

So, being ethical on your approach is the number one priority. Because, at the end of the day, your reputation will always be on the line.

CONTENT IS KING

We've all heard of this phrase, and we all get it. But, if we all understand this phrase, why is there still so much bad content out there?

At the end of the day, you need to provide value. If your information is common knowledge and invaluable, no one will follow you.

PLAN. PLAN. PLAN.

Before you start creating content, you should take the time to write out the topics of each title along with bullet points/highlights that you plan on addressing.

The easiest way to do this is to either create a series of episodes or simply write out all of the cool topics or subjects that are valuable.

Create catchy titles for them so that your audience will be excited to learn about it.

Your knowledge is extremely valuable, so take time to brainstorm and figure out what knowledge you contain that many wish they had. In addition, asking your audience can also help in this area.

RECORDING YOUR CONTENT

I've always believed in being authentic in your approach to content development and education. Never come off as scripted. That's not to say that scripts are bad. People are listening to you and your approach.

Show your personality and be animated. Have fun. But, don't *not* be you. Again, your audience will learn quickly if you are authentic or not.

When you record, the goal is to setup the video/podcast like a TV show by always addressing the subject of your current episode, offering solutions, and then leaving the show with a cliffhanger.

BEING CONSISTENT

How would you feel if your favorite TV show that aired at 7:00 p.m. just didn't air because the cast had to go watch a friend's baseball game?

Wouldn't that upset you?

You might not even continue to listen or view their shows anymore, right?

If you always have a show at a certain day and time, then make sure you air at that day and time at all costs.

HOW TO DISTRIBUTE

Your content needs to be re-purposed in several ways in order for your audience to find it.

- Record the video live or publish as though it's live on Facebook, YouTube, and Instagram.

- Remove the audio from the video using software such as Garage Band to prepare for podcasting.

- Transcribe the video by using rev.com. It's a paid service but well worth the investment.

Publish the video content on your personal Facebook page, then other outlets on Facebook such as a private group and your business page.

The video content that was transcribed will be slightly edited and posted on your website as a blog post. This editing simply allows the content to come out as though it's professionally written and not spoken.

When distributing on podcasting platforms, your best bet is to push it to some of the major players, such as iTunes and SoundCloud. You'll need to download software to help with the editing and preparation of this, such as GarageBand or Audacity.

Plus, make sure to use a media hosting company to host your podcasts to assist with smooth distribution.

Finally, if you are growing your email list, then you'll send an email blast to your list too.

WHO IS YOUR AUDIENCE?

You've got to know your audience. If you don't, then this chapter does you no good. Once you know who your audience is, make sure they are your friends on Facebook and Instagram, follow you, Like your business page, and join your private group.

This is how you create free content distribution.

Another strategy is to tag friends that rave about your content. Not all of them, but a good portion of them. This allows you to get free views from their friends who might also be interested in your topic.

To gain more followers and grow your email list, providing a lead magnet still works.

And, if you're good at Facebook marketing, that email list is gold. But, we won't get into that right now!

CAN'T STOP. WON'T STOP.

Okay—you need to make sure you continue to publish on a regular basis. Meaning, schedule your content and when it will be distributed. Every week.

And keep publishing. If you need to publish two to three times per week. Do it.

ABOUT JAVIER LOZANO, JR.

In 2001, Javier won a NASKA World Title in fighting and a Colorado State Title in 2000 and was one of the top competitors in the world.

With his early success, he decided to open a martial arts and personal training studio in August 2008—one month prior to the worst U.S. economic recession.

This made Javier become very intelligent and creative with digital marketing. In addition, he needed to create a sales system that closed at least 90% of prospects that came in.

After 5 years of continued growth, Javier expanded his studio by nearly 2x and grew gross sales to over $300k, while netting nearly 50% of revenue.

Javier has made well over $1 million running a professional studio, and decided to sell his lucrative business in February 2018 for a 6-figure payout.

He now owns and operates Bolder Media Solutions, a digital agency specializing in consulting and digital marketing for companies needing guidance in business growth, personal success, and domination in their market.

javier@boldermediasolutions.com
boldermediasolutions.com

NOTES

NOTES

FINDING FREEDOM, STAYING FREE

by Johnathan King

"Easiest way to deal with fear...turn it on itself. Fear not reaching
your goals. Fear not being all you can be."

-James Smiley

D oes this ring a bell? Were you like me and found yourself,
after years of experience in your industry, extremely talented,
but not as successful as you should be?

This was my life until I had coffee with James Smiley.

Times were extremely hard. I'll spare you the details, but believe
me, I was stressed and depressed.

Something needed to change. My personal life slowly got better,
but I needed to focus on my business now.

Looking for some sort of guidance, I decided to reach out to
James. We met at a Starbucks and began the conversation that would
change my life.

I've always tried to have a mentor and coach, and usually this was
my dad, a successful serial entrepreneur, but I needed someone who
knew exactly what I was trying to create, and that person was James.

He knew that I had quick success as a business owner at an early
age, a great ability to communicate with others, and a passion for
helping businesses grow. During the conversation, he handed me a
book and said "Bro, I want you to read this. You need to get into
consulting, man." That book was *DotCom Secrets* by Russell Brunson.

It was the book that changed everything. It made all of my confusion
become a victim to clarity and helped me create a strategy for success.

With James' help, I used strategies from his coaching to land my first few clients and began to scale.

Now to the good stuff.

A few months after I started my agency, I fell in love with a beautiful girl in Dallas who happened to be from Granada, Spain. Things got serious, and I boarded a plane and moved thousands of miles away.

This move forced me to find solutions for the obvious challenges. I could no longer meet with customers in person, and there was now a 7-hour time difference.

This challenge forced me to outsource 90% of the work necessary for my clients. Yes, 90%! This allowed me to find freedom from the stress of monitoring numerous Facebook ad accounts, handling sales, customer service, and everything else that comes with owning an agency. These solutions allowed me to grow and deliver better results for my clients as well.

So, you may be wondering how I did this. Prepare yourself; this is where it gets good.

1. FIND EXPERTS

I strategically sought out experts in very specific niches, agencies and individuals who focused on one skill or service. Not only do I use them to provide value to my clients, but I make sure I provide value to them as well. I have successfully and consistently done this with multiple well-known agencies and even have taught this method to other agencies.

2. AUTOMATION

While needing to become creative with a growth strategy, I also focused on tasks that I was performing daily that I could outsource. I found a great team of VAs and started testing projects. In the beginning, the majority of these projects were just list building, which led to my most successful cold outreach strategy to date.

3. AUTOMATED COLD OUTREACH

I spoke with Ankit, the owner of the VA agency, and told him I needed to find a way to automate what I was doing on Instagram. I was searching daily for specific business pages within a targeted niche and messaging them. Within 2 weeks I had set 12 appointments. I quickly realized that I didn't have time to find and message 20/30 pages every day, but my VA did.

By automating and implementing this system, we have generated nearly 6 figures in sales from Instagram this year. Here's why, the owners of these businesses are paying attention to their inboxes. The open rates and response rates are higher than any email I've sent. If you aren't utilizing Instagram to connect with your prospects, you are truly missing out.

I would ask that, if nothing else, you try this for yourself. Use hashtags to find pages in the industry that you serve. Send a message asking if you can send them more clients or business, and then make sure to follow up once a week until they tell you no or until they schedule a call with you. This works! Recently, we closed a deal with another prospect from Instagram with whom we had been following up for three months.

This is the power of automation and the power of attention. People are extremely overwhelmed with Facebook and text messages, emails go unread, but Instagram is an escape, so the attention is easier to grab there. Take action and grab it!

ABOUT JONATHAN KING

A graduate of Abilene Christian University and former multi-unit franchise owner, Johnathan has quickly gained the knowledge and experience to serve business owners.

After owning and selling multiple businesses, Johnathan began helping business owners better understand their purpose. With a focus on revenue-generating marketing techniques, he works closely with experts around the world to deliver custom solutions.

Johnathan takes pride in having a large and proven network of strategic partners to find solutions to many common problems experienced by mid to large-sized operations.

He currently resides in Granada Spain enjoying tapas, culture, and traveling with his fiancé.

jking@serveconsultant.com
serveconsultants.com

NOTES

NOTES

5 TIPS ON HOW MASTERING YOUR ONLINE REPUTATION WILL MAKE YOU THE LEADER IN YOUR INDUSTRY

by Jorge Cruz

A re your advertising efforts on pay-per-click, magazines, radio, or TV not yielding the increased sales you expected for your business? You might be ignoring one crucial factor: the status of your online reputation.

Your online reputation is the collection of what people are saying in the digital world about you, your products, services, and the experiences your business has provided. Online reputation is one of the most important (if not the most important) mental triggers that motivates people to take action. Why? Because, by human nature, people assume that if something works for somebody else, it will also work for them.

Most of the time, online reputation is shaped by online reviews. Research has found that 31% of people will trust ads, but 84% will trust reviews posted online as much as a personal recommendation from family and friends. Actually, 93% of people read reviews before making a purchase decision. These are statistics you can't ignore!

"People care more about another's experience than the price they will have to pay simply because this other person was in the same situation they are, and you are the solution for their problems. So, let your patients talk about you instead of you talking about your own services." That's what I said to one of my clients, a weight loss specialist who was dealing with some reputation issues a few years ago.

Nowadays, her business is the first result to appear in online search for her local area. Not only that, she has also achieved a huge business shift. Clients from all over the world contact her, not just "shopping" to evaluate if she can help them, but to secure the next available appointment.

I gave the same advice to a chiropractor who was referred to me just as he started his practice with a limited budget. In only two years, he opened a second office and was chosen as the chiropractor for international sporting events, including the 2016 Olympic Games in Rio.

HOW DID THESE CLIENTS SUCCEED?

By making their online reputation the cornerstone of their marketing strategy. Here are my top five tips on how you can do the same. http://RaiseYourReputation.com

ASK FOR REVIEWS IN A TIMELY MANNER

Did you know that 77% of people will give you a review if you ask for it? Ask for written reviews at the right moment. Make the approach in person when their pain has been relieved. Get their verbal commitment just before they leave your office. Then, you can either use automated software or printed cards to guide them in honoring their word.

VIDEO TESTIMONIALS ARE BETTER THAN WRITTEN REVIEWS

If written reviews are important, video testimonials are 10x more powerful! A video is more impactful because people easily relate to another human experience through body language and tone of voice. So, contact your happy clients and ask them for a short video testimonial. Also, provide them with a video release form that will allow you to market these videos all over the Internet.

PLACE YOUR REVIEWS WHERE YOUR PROSPECTS CAN FIND THEM

Directories are where your online reputation resides. You might be thinking only about Google or Yellow Pages but there are many more than that. Directories help your prospects find you easily and help you build social proof based on what your clients are posting on them. As everything online is public, make sure you claim, verify and optimize all the directories related to your business and niche. This will help you drive highly qualified traffic ready to pay you! List of directories: http://RaiseYourReputation.com

TURN NEGATIVES INTO POSITIVES

Even though negative experiences should be avoided, let's be honest, not all days are good days. If you see or feel your clients are dissatisfied, ask them how you can make it better. Don't let them leave your business until you are sure you put their concerns at ease.

If they already posted a negative comment online, don't be afraid to apologize. Respond wisely, focused not on the reviewer but on how your prospects would see you taking care of the situation in a caring and professional manner. A dissatisfied client will harm your reputation and could cost you thousands of dollars to fix.

PROVIDE EXCEPTIONAL SERVICE

Despite the fact that you might have a better strategy for collecting reviews from your clients, keep in mind that worthy reviews come from EXCEPTIONAL experiences. So, don't take your service for granted, and give your best at every step of the client journey. You won't believe how a caring doctor or a compassionate sales rep can impress clients, inspiring them to write positive reviews right away.

Your reputation is your most valuable asset, and you have no choice than to leverage it and avoid damaging it. Learn how: http://RaiseYourReputation.com

ABOUT JORGE CRUZ

Jorge Alberto Cruz is a passionate marketer with over 17 years of experience in traditional and digital marketing. His is the founder and owner of Marketing Innovations Group.

Jorge is an enthusiastic entrepreneur who is passionate about marketing psychology. He is focused on leveraging thousands of dollars and has multiple years in education on helping other entrepreneurs reach their marketing goals.

Jorge has helped hundreds of local and international companies like The Orlando Magic, The NBA, Texaco, Gulf, Gatorade, multiple physician practices, and other big companies achieve challenging projects.

For the last five years, Jorge has focused on helping doctors and medical practices develop their reputation online, speaking at seminars, and coaching business owners to innovate and squeeze the juice out of the Internet.

Jorge is a Hispanic leader and very proud of being Puerto Rican. He lives focused on his wife, four kids, and marketing the word of his most important client/boss—GOD

support@marketinginnovationsgroup.com
raiseyourreputation.com

NOTES

NOTES

HOW TO MAKE YOUR COMPETITION IRRELEVANT USING A FACEBOOK AD HACK MOST MARKETERS DON'T WANT YOU TO KNOW

by Kim Barrett

First of all, if you are reading this—congratulations. Everything in this book is designed to help you get the most out of your business, and this chapter will be no different.

You'll learn a simple strategy to implement to allow you to get the most out of Facebook, and it is so simple that most marketers don't want you to know it's even a possible answer to your problems. By the end of this chapter, you should have a fundamental understanding of how to apply this strategy to grow your business.

Let's get to it!

The first strategy you need to know is what I refer to as the N.O.C. This stands for Niche, Offer, Copy.

It sounds so simple, but let's take a deep dive into each of these.

NICHE.

Now, if you have been in business longer than a year, then you have probably devised some form of a niche. You know who you want to work with, what some of their characteristics are, and probably their age and location. When you are running ads, that is just not specific enough. Why?

Everything on Facebook is customized and curated. That's right, *everything*. Check it out. Ask someone close by to you to check out their Facebook account, and as you scroll, notice how it's completely different from yours. Notice how everything is customized and curated specifically to them. That's exactly how your marketing needs to be.

So, you need to customize and curate your marketing message specifically to your market.

Don't worry, listed below is the ideal framework for you to use to make sure you home in on your niche.

Age Range (10 years) – e.g. 25–35
Gender – Male or female
Location – City, state, country
Behaviors (list out 10) – What do they do, what actions do they take to solve their problems
Interests (list out 10) – Include TV shows, books, magazines, influencers they follow

If you follow the above framework, and you follow it to a tee, you will immediately start to see how this flows into the next two sections.

OFFER.

When you here offer, you probably are already thinking about irresistible offers, SLOs (self-liquidating offers) and all of that fun stuff.

Stop it.

You need to focus on what is so irresistible to your specific niche that they can't help but give you their email address. Because they need it. They don't just want it, but they *need* it. You've probably created offers before, but I challenge you to think about if it was really irresistible. Would you jump through your screen to enter your email/phone number/credit card?

If not, then you need to get back to the drawing board. Offer it to someone in your niche and see if they would push people out of the way to get access to it.

You need to identify their current situation and then show them what the Promised Land looks like. If you can do that, then you will never have a Facebook ad problem ever again. This is why these three parts all tie so perfectly together. Honing in and choosing a hyper specific niche means that you already have all the ammunition you need to articulate to that audience exactly what their problems are. Which leads us to the last step.

COPY.

Not looking over your partner's shoulder to copy the words off their page—but copywriting.

This is articulating to your specific niche your offer and enticing them to take action. Copywriting becomes easy when you have spent a few hours on the first two points. By understanding your specific niche's problems and sharing with them a solution, you can write like a six-year-old and still get leads. You don't have to be Gary Halbert to run Facebook ads, but you do have to put in the work. Put in the hours to understand your market.

Then, Facebook ads become easy.

You'll notice that nothing here has to do with the "technical" side of Facebook. That's because that stuff is easy; you can Google how to setup an ad. But what you just went through takes time, energy, and effort. Even though it's simple, it's the difference that makes the difference.

And now you have a measuring stick. If something is not working in a campaign you are running on any platform, simply look at the N.O.C.

Is there a problem with the Niche, Offer, or Copy?

You'll know pretty quickly which one it is.

This is how you make your competition irrelevant. By doing the work they don't want to do. By understanding your market better than anyone else. I guarantee, your results will skyrocket if you just do this one thing.

ABOUT KIM BARRETT

Kim Barrett is the founder of Your Social Voice, an online marketing and lead generation agency serving experts and business owners who want to scale online.

Kim got his start in the field of marketing fourteen years ago and has worked inside accounting firms, IT companies, and grain trading companies where he focused on growing profitability through better marketing strategies.

Using his expertise with Facebook ads and other online lead generation methods, Kim took his agency from zero to $100,000/month in sales in under a year.

He is an international bestselling author, speaker, and trainer and taught marketing around the world in 10 countries and 20 different industries. Kim helped many businesses grow from 6 to 7 and even 8 figures. As a direct result of his consulting and services, Kim added in excess of $10MM in sales to businesses around the world.

Some of Your Social Voice's clients have included ASX listed companies, and event marketing for Gary Vaynerchuk, Reese Witherspoon, and many other prominent speakers.

kim@yoursocialvoice.com.au
yoursocialvoice.com.au

NOTES

NOTES

THE 5 WAYS TO GROW ANY BUSINESS

by Manny Talavera

There are 28 million small businesses in the United States, and most business owners struggle. The reason they struggle is because they're not actually business owners. They're simply "technicians" in a business.

Most people get into a business based on a passion they have. A baker starts a bakery. A carpenter starts a remodeling company. And a florist starts a flower shop.

While they're great at that technical skill, in most cases they know nothing about lead generation, conversion, average transaction size, or lifetime value of a customer. They're trying to operate in a business environment without having the proper skills to do so.

There are five ways to grow a business, but if you ask the average business owner, most of them would have a difficult time articulating even one of them accurately.

The first way to grow a business is to increase leads. Increasing leads is all about getting a person to raise their hand and express interest in what you have to offer.

A person can do that by opting in, going to your website, calling you on the phone, or visiting your place of business. These are just some of the ways a person can take an action.

The second way to grow a business is increase conversions. Increasing conversions is all about getting more of those people who raised their hands and expressed interest to actually buy.

Most people who contact me for consulting are seeking more leads. In a lot of cases, they do not actually have a lead generation problem, they have a conversion problem.

They are simply not converting enough of the leads they are currently getting. Before increasing leads, we want to make sure the business owner is converting a good amount of the leads they are already getting.

So what businesses have about 100% conversion? If you said grocery stores and fast food restaurants, you would be right. Within reason, when people go into a fast food restaurant or grocery store, they are going to buy something.

Take Walmart, for example. They do not have a lead generation or a conversion problem. The average transaction size at a non-grocery store Walmart is $41.05. Walmart's goal is to get that transaction size up to $41.55.

Now a lot of you are wondering why Walmart would be interested in an extra $0.50 per transaction. The answer is simple. Walmart has 200 million customers. 200 million customers times $0.50 is $100 million dollars.

These customers all shop at Walmart an average of once per week or 52 times per year. $100 million dollars times 52 is just over $5 billion a year in additional revenue.

The third way to grow a business is increase average transaction size. Increasing average transaction size is getting the customer to spend more at the point of purchase. This is done by offering a variety of upsells and cross sells. Walmart does this simply by keeping people in the store longer. The longer they are in the store, the more they spend.

The fourth way to grow a business is to increase frequency of purchase. This is done by selling to your customers more often. One big problem is that many small business owners market to get a customer, and after that, they market to get a new customer and forget about the person who they just sold to.

It is actually nine times easier to get a customer to buy from you again than it is to get someone new to buy for the first time. Most customers quit buying from a business, not because of poor quality or service, but because they feel ignored.

The fifth way to grow a business is increase the lifetime value of a customer. Increasing the lifetime value of a customer is all about getting a person who might only buy once or twice and turning them into a lifetime customer.

This is done by constantly delivering value to the customer and reminding them how important they are to your business. All of the long-term money in any business is in the buyers list.

So, the five ways to grow a business are:

1. Increase leads

2. Increase conversions

3. Increase average transaction size

4. Increase frequency of purchase

5. Increase lifetime value

There are specific strategies for helping business owners do each one of these and the strategies will vary, based on the type of business, average transaction size and if the business is online or offline.

My goal as a marketing consultant is to take people out of the business they are in temporarily and put them in the marketing business. So the baker is not in the cake-making business but in the business of marketing cakes.

By focusing on the five ways to grow and build marketing systems that generate ongoing leads and conversions, this allows businesses to scale quickly and often attain geometric growth.

ABOUT MANNY TALAVERA

Manny Talavera received a degree in marketing, retail, and mid-management from Ball State University. He started his journey with USA Funds and worked with many Fortune 500 companies, including Verizon, Household Finance, and the Internal Revenue Service before going into business for himself.

Bitten by the entrepreneur bug, his first business venture was a 16-table pool room he bought with $10,000 he financed on credit cards. After that, he purchased and operated a lucrative hair salon with tanning beds and a thriving advertising publication before going on to becoming a marketing consultant.

Manny Talavera is a marketing consultant with a proven track record of helping people build and scale to the 7-figure mark. He has worked in the industry for over 14 years.

In addition to studying marketing and strategy for over 15,000 hours, he has also created over 50 products and courses, including his latest course, Marketing Consultant Mastery.

During his marketing career, he has worked with some of the greats including Glazer-Kennedy Inner Circle and Chet Holmes International. He currently divides his time between consulting and course creation.

NOTES

NOTES

THE FORGOTTEN SOCIAL MEDIA TECHNIQUE FOR MAKING MONEY

by Marcus Guiliano

Never before in our business culture have we been able to communicate as fast as we can with social media. These platforms give us an inexpensive prepared or uncensored message. There is so much to learn on this ever-evolving topic that people even pay for classes to get a competitive edge. We are all after more followers, more likes, more comments, and in some cases, a platform to sell online. The plan of attack is the usual: post content and then follow up with more and more content.

Let's take a step back and look at this a little differently. We all know communication is a two-way street. Social media is virtual communication. The same age-old principle applies. The bottom line is that it's communication, and you have to treat it as such.

Reflecting back, I can honestly say great communication is very rarely about me. It's about how I start the conversation to find out what is going on with someone else. Once I gave up the need to say what was important to me, I reversed it and gave them the opportunity to tell me things changed. But how often do we do this on social media? I want to share some specific tips that I have found to work successfully on social media.

LOOK FOR PEOPLE WHOSE ACTIVITIES ARE RELATED TO YOUR BUSINESS AND APPROACH THEM IN A FRIENDLY WAY.

The question has already been asked, and now it's your turn. There are people out there that are posting on topics that relate to your business. They might be buying or getting ready to buy a competitor's product. They might be reviewing a competitor's product. They might be asking a question to learn about a product or service that you could provide for them. But—and this is a very big but—you are not going in for the kill. You are going to engage in a conversation with them. You might provide them tips or tricks or just have friendly conversation.

This is about creating connections and relationships with current and potential clients. You are building trust and a community. For example, if you own a ski shop near a ski area, you should engage with local skiers. Instagram will show you who is posting and checking in. Just hit the "like" button or make a simple comment like, "Great day for skiing." You don't need to follow them. In fact, I wouldn't recommend following them. If they like your brand, they will follow you. And they might even stop in to pick up a pair of gloves or more.

COMMENT ON PEOPLE'S POSTS IN YOUR COMMUNITY AND MAKE THEM FEEL LIKE YOU ARE PAYING ATTENTION TO WHAT'S IMPORTANT TO THEM.

In my business as a restaurant owner, this is very effective tactic. I'm sure you can be creative and see what works for your business. This is a way to engage. By community, I mean your local city and online virtual community.

PEOPLE LIKE TO SHOW OFF WHAT IS GOING ON IN THEIR LIVES, AND A SIMPLE "LIKE" OR COMMENT CAN GO A LONG WAY.

We thrive on attention and approval. We need people's support and approval. We all like to feel important, and we developed that need in early childhood. It's a great feeling of gratification to know people are listening to you. Imagine your favorite restaurant owner giving a "like" or comment on your son's graduation or your first day out on golf course. Again, we are building relationships; it's not about a hard sell. In fact, it's very rarely about a hard sell.

RESPOND TO PEOPLE'S COMMENTS ON YOUR POSTS AND ANSWER THEIR QUESTIONS.

This is a basic action that is very often neglected. I see way too many businesses make a post and get comments that just sit there without the business every responding back. Some of these might be questions that need an answer. Even if it's not a question, it still needs a response.

When we post, the follow up is important. Don't stop halfway when you post. Your community will often respond to your original post, but it's not over just yet. Keep the conversation going. Keep engaging and show that you are listening. Not taking the time to continue to engage can and will turn off your community. Why should they comment when it falls on deaf ears?

TAKE INTO CONSIDERATION THEIR OPINION ABOUT YOU OR YOUR BUSINESS.

Social media is the main way your community provides feedback. It's a powerful tool to get opinions, good or bad. But some of us aren't sure how to handle a bad opinion or we overlook responding to a positive mention. This is where you have to treat review sites as social media as well. If someone takes the time to leave a comment or mention or review you, you should take the time to answer back.

Remember that all you want is to grow your business. The time spent on social media has to be just enough to use the above tips and give your business a boost. It doesn't have to be the main marketing strategy unless you are a big social media influencer. Keep track of what social media does for your business, but don't expect results right away. Sometimes it takes up to 15 times to touch a potential client with your brand.

ABOUT MARCUS GUILIANO

Marcus Guiliano is not necessarily your typical chef. Yes, he cooks. Yes, he creates. Yes, he understands and does what almost all chefs do. However, the difference is that Marcus is a chef, restaurant consultant, and professional speaker all in one. He is a serious advocate for helping other restaurants succeed and loves telling his personal journey about it all.

During his time both as a restaurateur and entrepreneur, Marcus has become a marketing expert. Marcus won an international marketing contest in 2008. Marcus has become a guest database expert focusing on educational marketing outreach combined with unique special event offerings. This combination of database management and analysis along with marketing outreach and regular communication with guests both old and new has resulted in building a successful destination restaurant in a small town.

Marcus's knowledge and experience regarding the nuts and bolts aspect of running a successful restaurant has been turned into a successful website/blog and consulting/cyber-coaching venture titled, *50 Mistakes Restaurant Owners Make* (www.50Mistakes.com).

Marcus is an international professional speaker and TEDx presenter. Marcus can inspire any crowd on business development, green business practices, and finding passion in your work.

marcus@marcusguiliano.com
marcusguiliano.com

NOTES

NOTES

5X YOUR AGENCY'S REVENUES BY LEVERAGING OTHERS

by Phillip Caillavet

C oming from the network marketing industry into the online consulting world, I took with me many systems and methodologies such as tap-rooting, which is using other people's warm markets so I never have to play in the cold market, as well as gamifying the prospecting process by keeping track of all the no's that I received until I finally got that yes, knowing that every time someone told me no, it was like putting money in my pocket.

I took away a lot more, but nothing more so than leverage. I've grown my own agency, Rebel Yell's, influence and income by leveraging other start-up agencies.

These newer agencies would go prospect, hustle hard, and sign new clients, but had no way of fulfilling the work efficiently and at the right cost to be able to make good profit margins themselves.

Being an extrovert and tapping into my network, I was able to find low-hanging-fruit clients and quickly go from zero to $30K a month in recurring revenue. Don't get me wrong, this was a huge accomplishment, but by leveraging the hustle of more than 20 start-up agencies and consultants for marketing and prospecting and our agency, Rebel Yell, providing wholesale fulfillment services for them, we were able to break the coveted 6-figure per month revenue mark.

This model allows us to spend 90% less on our own marketing to bring in new clients because we have others bringing them to us.

This white-label" joint venture model is easy to tap into if you provide a particular service or concentrate on a specific niche. Don't be greedy, and allow all parties involved to win and make money. Don't jump over the dimes to get to the dollars. Our motto is "Quality and Quantity."

ABOUT PHILLIP CAILLAVET

Who is Phillip Caillavet? Online Marketing Professional, Local Business Builder, Servant Leader.

I was first introduced to the online marketing Industry back in the 2008 and have been engrossed with it ever since.

I love online marketing because it offers the chance for anyone to create positive financial growth with little formal experience and little to no capital risk. And, I believe, "Success in online marketing is directly related to the degree in which one can give to others without the expectation of getting something in return."

Stand out from the crowd! I can't stop; I won't stop. Action. Action. Action.

phillip@rebelyell.co
rebelyell.agency

NOTES

NOTES

HOW AUTHENTICITY BUILDS EMPIRES (THE 3 KEYS TO YOUR AUTHENTICITY UNLOCKING UNSTOPPABLE BUSINESS GROWTH)

by Samuel Hodgett

Authenticity is, in my opinion, the key to building empires. I'm like most of you. I grew up with a burning (sometimes subconscious) desire to be an entrepreneur.

At the age of 12, my father finally went out on his own and started his own business. He instantly became my model of success. But what made him successful and grow his business so quickly was his authenticity and the relationships he had built up until that point.

He opened up a machine shop. But before he did, he spent more than five years working at someone else's machine shop. He learned the trade, interacted with the customers, and saw how the business was run. He built relationships with suppliers, machinists, and other people in the industry.

And most importantly, he was real. And because of his real-ness (or authenticity), people liked him. They trusted him. It was easy for them to do business with him.

AUTHENTICITY: MAKING IT EASY FOR PEOPLE TO DO BUSINESS WITH YOU

Now, you have to understand, as an extrovert, it's easy for me to be sociable with people and have a sense of how people perceive me. I can't teach you that.

As you continue to read, just know that I'm assuming you have the ability (or desire, at least) to be sociable with people, and even if it's not natural, to push yourself into the right situations and connections.

You see, authenticity happens within the context of connection, of relationship. And, in this day and age, people are smart. I believe people are now more perceptive of motive and drive.

There are too many charlatans in the world today, especially when it comes to the online business world. Too many opportunities that often are too good to be true.

So, what is true? What works for you? For me?

BE AUTHENTIC AND THEY WILL COME

Here it is. This is the secret.

This is how I was able to build multiple six-figure businesses, even in industries where I didn't have years of experience or layers of deep connections already.

The secret is: BE YOURSELF.

That, truly, is what it means to be authentic. Just be yourself.

Oh, so that one guy in that one Facebook ad is saying you can make $10k by "selling" Facebook ads to "easy clients?" Well, not everyone can authentically become an advertising specialist (or build an ad agency).

Oh, so that other lady in that YouTube ad said that all you had to do was build an Instagram account to 100k followers, and you're an instant celebrity? Well, not everyone can authentically balance the artistic and scientific skills it takes to actually be a successful Instagram influencer.

What works for one person rarely ever works for another, at least not in a copy and paste "just do what I do, and you'll win" sort of way.

TAKE IT, TWEAK IT, MAKE IT YOUR OWN

One of my mentors, Troy Dean, says this all the time in his program for WordPress experts, WP Elevation.

What I realized was that although these people experienced success and were giving others a roadmap to follow based on their success, what most people don't realize is that you can't just do it that way, fill in the blanks, and expect to see success.

That's one of the main drivers in our mastermind community, The Christian Entrepreneur Academy. We help 5 and 6-figure faith-based coaches, consultants, and service providers scale their businesses into multiple 6 and 7 figures.

But we don't do that by simply saying, "Here's how we did it; just copy us, and you'll be fine."

We provide guidance, and some direction, but mostly community and coaching.

In fact, we have members that do what we do—better. But they understand and appreciate the value of community and authenticity.

BE THE BEST VERSION OF YOU

Don't settle for simply copying someone else's formula thinking it will just work for you without making it your own. (That also means don't steal!)

Be you. Be your best. Let others know who *you* are.

And be real. Authenticity means you're not just showing people your good side.

The mentors in my life whom I value the most (like James Smiley) are the ones who are real. They share their pain and struggling just as much as they share their wins.

Don't hide behind a professional portrait and some crazy graphics. Don't hide behind the lights and the makeup.

Let the world see you. The real you. The only you.

The best version of you.

Be authentic.

ABOUT SAMUEL HODGETT

Sam Hodgett is a life-long entrepreneur. Born in rural Wisconsin, Sam grew up working in his father's business. Realizing his entire family was full of entrepreneurs, it wasn't long before he realized his fate… and his entrepreneurial calling was sealed.

He also grew up a Christian, and his faith was a major part of his life. He is on a life-long journey to discover the balance of his "ministry" calling with his "entrepreneur" calling.

Currently, he is the co-founder Smart Web Ninja, a business that helps online businesses scale into seven figures and beyond through comprehensive online sales & marketing automation campaigns. Recently, Smart Web Ninja became one of the very few Certified Partners with Digital Marketer.

Sam is also the co-founder of The Christian Entrepreneur Academy, the leading online community for faith-based entrepreneurs wanting to start and scale their coaching, consulting or device-based business. Through coaching, education, and community, their goal is to change the world through "Legacy-Businesses" and already have thousands of people in their community. As a special offer to book readers, you can join their Academy today for just $1! Just visit thechristianentrepreneuracademy.com to learn more today!

sam@yourfunnelninja.com
yourfunnelninja.com

NOTES

NOTES

RETARGETING FOR RICHES

by Sema Erzouki

You know this feeling all too well.

You are mindlessly scrolling on Facebook and see an ad that piques your interest. You choose not to enter your name or email or to click "purchase" and instead you X out of the screen.

But then you feel like you are being followed.

You see the same guy all over the Internet. His face is on a YouTube ad, in a Buzzfeed article you are reading, or even in Tinder ads!

Or, you were browsing Amazon for a new camera and then life got in the way so you forgot to complete your purchase.

You click back to Facebook, and voilà, there's an Amazon ad reminding you about that camera.

The temptation seeps in and you go back and complete your purchase.

This approach is called RETARGETING.

Experienced marketers like me are salivating over the power of retargeting. It allows us the ability to re-engage existing traffic educate them more on why they should buy our offers.

It also helps us stay connected with our existing traffic to maintain our brand's visibility and to promote new offers to our existing client base.

Retargeting can be as simple or as complex as you want it to be.

In this chapter, I'll walk you behind the scenes of my four easy Ad Retargeting strategies. I use these strategies with my clients to build their brands and create easy conversions on autopilot.

STRATEGY #1: CREDIBILITY RETARGETING

It may seem like a no-brainer, but before we make a buying decision, we must first know if you are credible.

The main reason we say yes to an offer is because we want it to solve our problem or get us closer to our desires.

What we must do as business owners is showcase our expertise and stand out from our competitors.

The strongest way to stand out as the #1 choice is through credibility retargeting.

If one of my clients gets featured on a blog, podcast, or TV segment, I run an ad to show their existing audience (buyers and nonbuyers). With this ad, there isn't a call to action. It's low cost and has a high impact in strengthening your positioning as an authority and keeping you top of mind.

STRATEGY #2: BRAND AWARENESS RETARGETING

Think about marketing as if it were dating. The quickest way to get rejected is to rush into closing the deal.

Asking to marry someone before the first date is over is too abrupt.

Don't make this same mistake with your ads. You need to provide value. This becomes crucial when you are building a funnel for cold audiences.

Instead, remember that slow and steady always wins the race, and in this case, the race equals higher ROI.

For this strategy, ease customers into your relationship with you.

When they first get on your email list or hit your website, hit them with a brand awareness ad that introduces you to your audience. A great way to do this is to use a video ad for your first ad, as it gives you a great medium to tell your brand's story.

Sure, some may click and convert immediately, but there's a good chance many won't.

That's fine if they don't because you can run a retargeting campaign that shows your ad to users who saved or engaged with your previous ad. After you follow up with a retargeting ad, you can focus on conversions or lead generation.

I also use this strategy to retarget with content such as blogs and videos. The more valuable the content you put out to your audience, the better your positioning and the more your audience trusts you.

This is important because your audience is filled with potential brand advocates that will proclaim your brand to high mountain tops if they feel valued.

STRATEGY #3: FOLLOW UP AND REMOVE OBJECTIONS

Do you remember the last time you were tempted to splurge on yourself but held off?

You might've been sticking to a budget, and you may have initially resisted the item at first.

But then it pops up in your Facebook feed, it feels like destiny, it's too good to pass up, and you buy.

You can use this strategy, too, for your own business!

When customers have visited specific pages of your site, it indicates strong interest and purchase intent.

There will be times where someone checks out your sales page and then exits without buying for of a range of reasons.

This type of traffic is SUPER hot and almost ready to buy.

You've already taken the time to get these people into your funnel, and now you need to close the deal.

They might just have a question to ask, or they might need to see a little bit of social proof before they are ready to buy.

In my experience, this is where I get the highest ROI for my clients. It's where you can put a few dollars in and get hundreds back.

To make this strategy effective, target users who visit specific pages, but exclude those who made a purchase. You can do this by excluding users who visited your order confirmation page.

We are pushing indecisive shoppers or forgetful viewers to convert. This is an enormous amount of untapped revenue for almost all businesses.

An added bonus that works with this strategy is to retarget them with a testimonial, give them a discount, or invite them to ask their question.

I've seen Messenger bots used as a center for FAQs, and they can generate serious returns when put into action.

STRATEGY #4: UPSELL RETARGETING

Don't neglect this crucial one!

The cost to gain a new customer is way more than the cost to keep a customer.

The best way to increase your average cart value is by presenting a buyer with an offer that complements or enhances what they bought.

Let's say you are a Facebook Ads agency, and you sold them on a retainer package. What are some other needs they might want? Do they also need social media management? Or a website redone?

By knowing your audience's desires, it becomes a no-brainer to offer them more value.

Regardless of which retargeting approach you take, the most important takeaway is that it is powerful to be omnipresent in your marketing and to follow up with potential customers. Use these strategies to stay top of mind in your industry and convert more sales.

Which retargeting strategy will you implement first?

ABOUT SEMA ERZOUKI

Sema grew up in an entrepreneurial household, and after graduating college, she decided that the traditional route of working a 9–5 job wasn't the direction she wanted to go. She wanted to start her own business, no matter how much work it took. After a few years of trial and error as an entrepreneur, she ended up falling in love with marketing, so she started her own ad agency helping businesses generate leads and convert those leads into paying customers. She now has a successful business working with 6 and 7-figure entrepreneurs helping them grow and scale their online courses and coaching programs. She has been behind the scenes of many 6-figure launches and has managed hundreds of thousands of dollars in adspend and generated millions in revenue for her clients.

Outside of business, Sema loves traveling, is an avid sports fan, and loves networking with others.

sema@semaerzouki.com
semaerzouki.com

NOTES

ESTABLISHING YOUR PRESENCE ONLINE

by Stephen Hauter

WHY YOU NEED TO KNOW WHO YOU ARE AND UNDERSTAND YOUR TRUE PASSION.

> "If you don't know where you are going,
> any road can take you there."
>
> - Lewis Carroll, *Alice in Wonderland*

- Tips on how to identify who you are:

- What do you want out of life?

- What/who is truly important to you?

- What are your values and beliefs?

- What do you want to protect on your journey as an entrepreneur?

- Who are some role models that have achieved goals similar to yours?

WHY YOU NEED TO KNOW WHO YOU ARE.

The biggest question is always how to get to success while expending the least amount of time and money. Ultimately, you'll need to understand and leverage your strengths so you don't waste resources chasing down your weaknesses. To do this, let's get grounded in one thing before applying anything else; you need to be true to yourself. Embrace your quirks. You can follow any line of research: marketing, emotional intelligence, or biblical references, and you'll find evidence that people (the ones buying the solution you have to solve their problems) want to associate with people who are authentic. You need to know who you are, and then be that person consistently across all avenues, social media, your individual pursuits, how you are with your family, and also in the solutions you bring to your customers.

Example to follow: When I was in the process of closing down the first soccer stores I opened, I took a job selling mortgage loans. While it appeared to be a good step to provide for my family, it was tough to become enthusiastic about the work. Ultimately, my wife and I decided it would be best for me to focus on my true passion, coaching soccer. From there, I took multiple coaching courses, including getting the USSF "A" and National Youth License, among others. This was the first step leading to starting my online membership site dedicated to soccer coaches, CoachingSoccerMadeSimple.com.

Knowing who you are influences every decision you make. It guides the company you keep, how you spend your money, the clothes you wear, the vehicle you drive, and where you live. Sometimes, we look around to see what others are doing, and you certainly want to do your research, but you always want to make the decision that best aligns with your person.

So, for Alice in Wonderland, if you don't know who you are, then you'll do anything. That creates cognitive dissonance or inconsistency for yourself that is unsettling. You'll have peace in your journey and go down less rabbit trails of distractions when you know who you are and what your goal is and have identified a plan to get there. Once you've done that, you can determine who can help you with that and can allocate your time and invest properly. I've noticed when I am clear on my path and allocate my time accordingly, there is so much joy in being present in that moment. Anxiety comes when I'm trying to do more than one thing at once (the folly of multitasking) or when I feel that I "should be" doing something else. Developing a plan that you can execute and then following through on that plan allows you to feel progress and success on a daily basis. This will keep you going.

"Success is the progressive realization of a worthy goal or ideal"

- Earl Nightingale

Singlemindedness is key. Going back and forth in your mind is an unhealthy, unproductive way to spend your mental energy. Knowing who you are can aid productivity in more ways than one.

Next Steps: After I launched my membership site, the next step was to provide products for the coaches, in my case, a soccer notebook. With over 27 years of coaching experience, I hoped to design a notebook for use on the sidelines that was dialed in to a coach's needs. This design was validated with quick and steady sales.

While I've been fortunate in having a clear vision for my passion and pursuing that from a young age, the membership site is most recent. And, you can begin at any age. Rely on your vision for direction. You can't expect others to validate your dream when they do not have the self-awareness you do.

"You have to understand your own personal DNA.
Don't do things because I do them or Steve Jobs
or Mark Cuban tried it. You need to know
your personal brand and stay true to it."

– Gary Vaynerchuk

ABOUT STEPHEN HAUTER

Stephen is married with three children and lives in Ohio. He has spent over 27 years playing, coaching, and training soccer. Stephen also holds a USSF "A" and National Youth License, NSCAA Director Of Coaching diploma, and is an instructor for USSF Coaching Licensing. Most importantly, Stephen is committed to developing the player on and off the field to succeed in LIFE and there is no better way to do that than soccer.

Stephen is also the State Director of Ohio for the Genova International School of Soccer which has helped over 80 American players sign professional soccer contracts in three years. It is available for boys and girls as well.

NOTES

NOTES

THE SECRET TO RETAINING CLIENTS WITHOUT A LOT OF WORK

by Zach Winsett

C lient retention is something that many people never discuss, but it is imperative to master if you want to have a successful agency. If your clients only stick around for two to three months, you will be forced to hustle to acquire new clients just to keep your level of revenue the same. The hustle and the stress to obtain new clients will eventually burn you out. If you can retain your clients, you simply build your revenue with each new client you obtain.

The techniques and systems that I personally use have resulted in clients sticking with me for over three years. Now, think about that for a minute. How much would a client be worth if you can get them to pay you for over three years? If the client is paying you $1k per month, that is $36k over the span of three years.

SECRET 1: GETTING RESULTS

Clients will not stick around unless you are delivering the results that were discussed when they agreed to work with you. It is very important to know the expectations of the client and to deliver what you promise. For example, I primarily use Google AdWords to generate leads for local contractors and service providers. On the discovery call with the client, I am sure to get several key pieces of information such the number of phone calls the client expects within a week or month. Once you have Google ads performing and leads are coming through, you can switch the client's account into maintenance mode. This means that you need to perform weekly management with the account and switch out of the setup phase. I have Google AdWords ads that have been running since the day I set them up, over three years ago. The client is very happy with the results, and I rarely hear from the client unless I reach out. What I have noticed is that, unlike Facebook, Google ads are more consistent, and you do not have to change out your ads as often as other platforms. This is because Google AdWords is based on keyword searches within a geographical area and not interest groups.

SECRET 2: TRACKING RESULTS

In order to retain your clients, you will need to be able to not only generate results, but you will need to prove your results. I use call tracking on every campaign I launch for a client. Currently, I am using CallRail, and it has saved me a ton of time with call reports. I have CallRail set up to send the client a weekly report of all phone calls generated, and I also send the client a monthly report. It only takes approximately two minutes to set up, and that is all. The system will email the client the reports automatically. Having a call tracking platform builds trust and shows transparency with your clients. I have several clients that want to view the AdWords account and monitor the adspend vs. clicks. I am completely open to sharing all data and results with my clients. Honesty and transparency speak volumes even if you are still struggling with generating results. All of my clients are month to month, and I do not make them sign long-term contracts. They stick with me for years because of the amount of value and trust I deliver.

SECRET 3: COMMUNICATION

Don't be afraid to call your clients to see how things are going. Yes, that means pick up the phone and have a conversation. Make an effort to reach out to your clients once per month. If you can't reach the client, then leave a voicemail that says "Hey this is X from XYZ, I am just checking in with you to see how things are going. I noticed that I was able to generate X phone calls, and I just wanted to see how many you were able to convert. Please give me a call back at your earliest convenience at XXX-XXX-XXXX." You will be surprised at how a small voicemail can build confidence in the client that you are taking care of them and you actually care.

So there you have it, the three secrets I use to retain clients. It's not rocket science, but I am confident that if you implement all three secrets into your business, you will see client retention skyrocket. If you have questions about client retention, lead generation, or ad platforms, you can reach out to me on Facebook.

ABOUT ZACH WINSETT

Zach Winsett is CEO/Founder of business consulting company, Strategic Digital Consultants, Inc. His company focuses on increasing the revenue of businesses by leveraging the Internet. Zach has produced over 30,000 leads for businesses using online ad platforms within the past two years. Client retention is the top priority of his company and providing services that make a difference to his client's bottom line. His primary strategy for producing leads is from using pay-per-click advertising. Zach also has two ecommerce brands that have produced over $500k in revenue within the first two years. He has coached many people to also produce profitable online stores utilizing Facebook ads and drop-shipping products. He has sourced successful products from international sources.

Before starting his online marketing journey, Zach served as the IT Manager for several software development companies in the Atlanta area. He also served as the project manager for five data center relocations. In 2015, Zach became a full-time business owner and online entrepreneur.

In his free time, Zach enjoys spending time outdoors and traveling with his family. He resides in the Atlanta area with his wife and son.

NOTES

39543472R00122

Made in the USA
Lexington, KY
20 May 2019